Working with Victims of Crime

Good Practice in Working with Violence
Edited by Hazel Kemshall and Jacki Pritchard
ISBN 1 85302 641 7

Good Practice in Risk Assessment 1
Edited by Hazel Kemshall and Jacki Pritchard
ISBN 1 85302 338 8

Good Practice in Risk Assessment 2
Key Themes for Protection , Rights and Responsibilities
Edited by Hazel Kemshall and Jacki Pritchard
ISBN 1 85302 441 4

Good Practice in Counselling People Who Have Been Abused
Edited by Zetta Bear
ISBN 1 85302 424 4

Competence in Social Work Practice
Kieran O'Hagan
ISBN 1 85302 332 9

Good Practice in Child Protection
A Manual for Professionals
Edited by Hilary Owen and Jacki Pritchard
ISBN 1 85302 205 5

Managing Child Sexual Abuse Cases
Brian Corby
ISBN 1 85302 593 3

Sexual Abuse
The Child's Voice – Poppies on the Rubbish Heap
Madge Bray
ISBN 1 85302 487 2

Invisible Victims
Crime and Abuse Against People with Learning Disabilities
Christopher Williams
ISBN 1 85302 309 4

Working with Victims of Crime

Policies, Politics and Practice

Brian Williams

Jessica Kingsley Publishers
London and Philadelphia

The right of Brian Williams to be identified as author of this work has been asserted by him in accordance with the Copyright, Designs and Patents Act 1988.

First published in the United Kingdom in 1999 by
Jessica Kingsley Publishers Ltd
116 Pentonville Road
London N1 9JB, England
and
325 Chestnut Street
Philadelphia, PA 19106, USA.
www.jkp.com

Copyright © 1999 Brian Williams

Library of Congress Cataloging in Publication Data
A CIP catalogue record for this book is available from the Library of Congress

British Library Cataloguing in Publication Data
Williams, Brian
Working with victims of crime: policies, politics and practice
1.Victims of crimes - Services for
I.Title
362.8'8

ISBN 1 85302 450 3

Printed and Bound in Great Britain by
Athenaeum Press, Gateshead, Tyne and Wear

Contents

ACKNOWLEDGEMENTS   6

1. Introduction   7

2. Repeated Criminal Victimisation   23

3. The Needs of Victims of Crime   51

4. The Politics of Victimisation   67

5. Who Helps Victims?   89

6. The Way Forward   123

    APPENDIX   139
    REFERENCES   145
    INDEX   157

Acknowledgements

Many people have helped with the research for this book by allowing me to interview them, by responding to requests for information and by discussing their ideas with me. There are too many to name them all individually but I would like to mention some people who went out of their way to help. Dr Denis Bracken and Jane Ursel of the University of Manitoba and Larry Kroeker advised on the Canadian criminal justice system, answered endless questions and supplied invaluable reference material. In the UK the staff and volunteers of Victim Support, Rape Crisis and SAMM were patient, enthusiastic and helpful in agreeing to be interviewed and in answering questions by telephone and by post. Inspector Trevor Hood of Staffordshire Police gave me considerable help with the case study in Chapter Five.

The book is built upon previous research undertaken with Mike Kosh, Hilary Nettleton and Professor Sandra Walklate. All were a pleasure to work with and I owe them a great deal. Dr Jacky Smith did a good deal to stimulate my original interest in work with victims of crime, as did Tony Brewerton, and I was greatly helped by discussions with Paul Kingston, Sue Roberts and Azrini Wahidin at various stages.

Staff in the libraries at Cambridge University Institute of Criminology, De Montfort University (Scraptoft campus), Keele University and Southampton University have been unfailingly helpful, particularly the Inter-Library Loans staff and Phil Johnson at Keele, as have the long-suffering computer support staff at De Montfort. I would also like to acknowledge the hospitality and friendship of Kate Rose and Dominic Amans, and to thank Jim for all the walks.

Finally, thanks to Suzanne Wright for taking such an interest in the book, and for her constant support.

Brian Williams
Leicester, January 1999

CHAPTER ONE

Introduction

The needs and rights of victims of crime have attracted increasing political and professional interest since the early 1970s. Then, there was a vague feeling that more could be done to improve victims' lot and a range of small interest groups was formed to achieve this. Now, there is a much wider variety of voluntary organisations dedicated to supporting victims and, to a greater or lesser extent, committed to campaigning for improvements in their situation. Policies at national and local levels have been changed in recognition of victims' needs, an increasingly distinct academic discipline of victimology has emerged and the caring and policing professions have increasingly changed their practices so as to address issues of victimisation more effectively. Nevertheless, much remains to be done and greater attention to the position of victims has revealed unmet needs.

Along the way, victims' issues have become increasingly politicised in North America and, later, in Europe and other parts of the world. There is a corresponding need for objective information about criminal victimisation: how can victims best be helped, what are their needs, what rights do they and should they have?

This book is designed to meet the need for that information. It begins by outlining the developments described above, in the UK and elsewhere, and goes on to look at some of the questions raised by the rise of a victims' movement and of political and professional concern about victims of crime. It then addresses issues specific to particular types of crime.

It is intended to be useful to readers with an interest in social policy and criminology, as well as people involved in planning and providing direct services to victims and in the training of those who provide such services. At the policy level it examines the reasons for the increasing prominence of issues around victimisation and the nature and composition of the organisations set up to provide services to victims. Where appropriate, developments in the UK are compared with initiatives and experiments in other countries. The political response to pressure for improved treatment of victims is then analysed: the Victim's Charter is used as a case study of government responses to campaigns for new services in England and Wales. It is argued that the whole Citizen's Charter initiative is designed to individualise social problems, detracting attention from their underlying causes, and that while the Victim's Charter has led to improvements in services, it has a number of underlying political purposes which have little to do with the needs of victims of crime.

Many developments affecting victims of crime in Europe echo previous events in North America, and for that reason alone it is worth paying attention to the American experience. However, the American legal system is very different both from European systems and from those of its neighbours. The various European legal systems differ considerably from each other in their philosophy and organisation. These differences are often revealing and may lead one to challenge one's preconceptions about how things should be done. The book therefore takes a comparative approach to many of the questions discussed.

Alongside this big picture, the book sets the practical issues involved in helping victims and arguing their individual cases for receiving resources and services. How do people react to victimisation and how can professional and voluntary service providers help them towards recovery? What is the role of each of the agencies involved in supporting victims? How might the criminal justice system improve its service to victims?

Outline of the book

The remainder of this chapter looks at the rise of victims' organisations, the politicisation of victims' issues and the unfortunate legacy of academic victimology (which, in its early days, tended unintentionally to stereotype victims or even to blame them for their victimisation). It also briefly discusses some terminological issues: why, for example, do some victims prefer to be described as survivors?

Chapter Two traces a continuity between victim blaming and later academic concern to understand why some people suffer repeated victimisation. Is political and research attention to the fact that some people become victims over and over again distracting us from examining possible structural reasons for the vulnerability of those who are repeatedly victimised? In order to analyse the over-representation of some individuals in victimisation statistics, the extent to which members of particular social groups may appear in the figures is considered. Do such variables as gender, race, class or disability interact with poverty and lack of opportunities to explain the concentration of victimisation in particular areas and groups? Here, and throughout the book, case examples are used to illustrate the issues. These are drawn from real cases, but disguised in order to protect the anonymity of the people concerned.

In Chapter Three the needs and responses of the victims of some particular types of crime are reviewed. While there is no way of predicting how an individual will react, there is an increasing body of knowledge relating to the range of likely responses to specific types of harm. Burglary, murder and rape are examined, again using case examples and relating these to the theoretical literature. Burglary is one of the most common offences referred to Victim Support schemes and a case example allows issues raised by other relatively minor offences to be considered. Although murder and rape are much less common than burglary, the experience of those who survive rape, and those who are left behind after a murder, illustrate some of the difficulties caused for victims by the way they are treated by the criminal justice system.

Chapter Four returns to the politics of victimisation and develops the argument, outlined later in this chapter, about the extent to which policy in relation to victims is made with a view to neutralising the anger and potential power of an emerging victims' movement. This has consequences in terms of the actual treatment that individual victims receive. Was the Victim's Charter a step in the right direction or a false start in terms of creating a culture of recognition of victims' rights? There is a corresponding dilemma for the agencies and individuals involved in supporting victims at a local level: how can individuals' needs be met without losing sight of the policy and resource implications? While each victim must clearly be supported in a caring and effective manner, the need for procedural and political change is also evident when dealing with individual cases. The agencies working with victims have to strike a balance between their one-to-one work and a wider advocacy role. Volunteers' views on the best way of managing this tension are drawn upon in the discussion.

A range of organisations exists to meet victims' needs, ensure they get their rights and argue for these rights to be extended. Throughout the book examples are drawn from the work of these different agencies. Chapter Five looks at some groups in more detail, including Victim Support, Rape Crisis, Women's Aid and Support After Murder and Manslaughter. Once again, case studies are used, this time in order to illustrate good practice. The chapter goes on to describe the ways in which the different groups work together and to suggest possible approaches to improving relationships between them.

Finally, Chapter Six concludes the book by discussing the future of support for victims of crime. How can we give victims genuine choices? How can services, and liaison between them, be enhanced? The implications of the individual and agency case studies in earlier chapters for future policy are addressed, with a view to suggesting positive policy changes for the future.

The birth of a victims' movement

There is room for argument about whether victims of crime – whose status as such is temporary and, in many less serious cases, soon forgotten – represent a new social movement (see Chapter Six). What is quite clear, however, is that they and the agencies set up to help them have become increasingly influential over the period since the early 1970s (when Britain's first Women's Aid refuge was set up in Chiswick, London, and Victim Support was founded in Bristol).

The example of Victim Support shows how this influence has been built up. The history of this organisation illustrates the growth of the wider victims' movement (see Appendix (p.139) for the international context and for developments in other victim organisations). Victim Support started as a local initiative in one English city, drawing upon ideas from North America, and grew quite slowly. Nevertheless, it provided a model for similar projects in other parts of Europe and, once a pilot project was established, attracted considerable national and international interest. The idea was clearly one whose time had come.

The first development was the establishment of the Bristol Victims-Offenders Group in 1970. Out of this grew the National Victims' Association, founded in 1973, also in Bristol. It brought together victims in the local area and then set up an independent victim support scheme (which had to cease offering its services after only a few months, recognising the need for further fund-raising to support the high volume of work; it was relaunched in 1975). The second inauguration was much more successful, attracting national television coverage and the offer of administrative support from an existing national charity – the National Association for the Care and Resettlement of Offenders (NACRO). This soon led to the establishment of schemes in other areas, encouraged by a conference which promoted the idea, and to the creation of a national body in 1979. By 1980 there were 256 local schemes, receiving 125,000 referrals per year (Mawby and Walklate 1994). This increased to 360 schemes by 1995, with 800 staff and 16,000 volunteers. By then, Victim Support was offering assistance to more than a million victims each year and schemes were operating in all parts of the country (Victim Support 1996).

Parallel national schemes had also been set up in Scotland, Northern Ireland and the Republic of Ireland. As can be seen from the Appendix, these were fairly soon followed by the establishment of similar organisations in France and the Netherlands.

This represents a remarkable growth in the size and geographical coverage of a voluntary agency. A number of factors contributed to this rapid expansion. First, the relaunched Bristol project had secured the support of the police, probation and social services. Their staff became involved in volunteer training, providing administrative support, making referrals and, in some cases, fund-raising. This model was successfully adapted by projects in other parts of the country and formal representation of these agencies on the management committees of local schemes was required by Victim Support once it became established as a national body. Although the Home Office discouraged probation officers from becoming involved with Victim Support at first, there was a change of national policy in 1983. Victim Support was then held up as a model of the type of partnership which probation services should form with their local communities and the level of liaison and activity increased (Holtom and Raynor 1988).

These links with the local state made it easier for Victim Support to gain access to decision makers at national level. In 1987 Home Office funding was obtained for the first time. Initially provided for three years, this enabled the national umbrella body and some of its local schemes to employ staff to co-ordinate their work. The numbers of referrals increased rapidly, justifying further government funding, and this increased substantially between 1987 and 1995.

Meanwhile, schemes had begun to tackle new areas of work. At first, there had been a marked reluctance to become involved in supporting victims of more serious crime, especially in the case of sexual offences, murder and racial and 'domestic' violence. More advanced training was gradually provided for selected volunteers and some began to take on more serious cases. In London, for example, some schemes began to work with rape survivors in the early 1980s. Specialist training became available nationally from 1985 and the police began to make referrals systematically in rape cases at about the same time. Similarly, a pilot project was set up to examine the feasibility of providing support to the families of murder victims and a strong case was made for taking on this work (Brown, Christie and Morris 1990). Once again, specialist training was devised and offered, and many local schemes now respond to this need. Some families have reported finding Victim Support volunteers 'out of their depth' when undertaking this work and some have found small, self-help organisations, such as Parents of Murdered Children, more congenial (Brown 1993). Nevertheless, a valuable new service is clearly being provided by Victim Support schemes in many areas.

A further growth area has been the provision of support to witnesses before and during their court appearances. Once again, Victim Support commissioned a pilot study – which found that the experience of giving evidence was a traumatic one for many victims and other witnesses (NAVSS 1988; Raine and Walker 1990). The provision of services such as a separate waiting room, a chance to see the lay-out of an empty court, explanatory leaflets and the support of a sympathetic volunteer made a considerable difference to the way witnesses experienced court attendance. Over the next six years, coverage of all Crown Courts in England and Wales was gradually achieved and the schemes are now being extended to cover Scotland and some busy magistrates' courts (Victim Support 1996).

Another reason often given for the growth of Victim Support, and its central-government funding, is its studied neutrality on political issues. From the beginning there was a careful avoidance of comment on matters relating to the sentencing of offenders and on wider political issues of concern to victims of crime. It was thought that intervention on such issues would divide the membership of the organisation and cause unnecessary friction with other partner agencies, which would not serve the interests of victims well (Holtom and Raynor 1988). Although the national organisation gradually became more confident about giving evidence to government committees, preparing press releases on issues of the day and commenting on specific policies and proposals, it continues to advise its staff and volunteers to avoid public comment on individual cases or on sentencing policy or practice. Victims' right to confidentiality overrides the potential benefit to the organisation of using their stories for publicity and fund-raising purposes (Newburn 1995).

As victims' issues have become more politicised and controversial, this neutral stance has been harder to maintain. Indeed, there are signs that Victim Support at national level has adjusted its strategy to take account of the changing climate. In 1995, for example, Victim Support published a policy paper entitled *The Rights of Victims of Crime* (Victim Support 1995). This was significant because the organisation had previously confined itself to making public statements mainly about the *needs* rather than the *rights* of victims. Although this may seem no more than a semantic distinction, the contents of the document confirm that Victim Support has begun to adopt a more assertive strategy. In addition to codifying what victims should be able to expect under existing arrangements, the paper identifies a large number of areas on which Victim Support argues that further work needs to be done by various criminal justice agencies and by central government.

It is, perhaps, significant that this assertion of independence on the part of Victim Support coincided almost exactly with the Home Office decision not to increase its funding for the period 1996–98, the first time since 1987 (Williams 1999). Of course, penal policy had also changed dramatically during that period and the cost of punitive sentencing policies was forcing the government to make cuts in other areas (Newburn 1995). Nevertheless, the strategy of political neutrality served the organisation well in its first two decades. By the 1995–96 financial year, it received £10.8 million of Home Office funding. While this represented only 0.1 per cent of the total criminal justice budget (Victim Support 1997), it was a significant amount by any standards.

The politicisation of victims' issues

Many commentators have bemoaned the increasing politicisation of victims' issues. Political interest in an issue can be good news for those interested in it, raising the profile of social problems and attracting resources to the effort to alleviate them, but it is not always so. Where crime victims are concerned, a higher political profile has certainly led to the allocation of additional resources, as the brief history of Victim Support above confirms. However, there is room for doubt about politicians' motives in drawing attention to victims, and the solutions they offer to the problems surrounding criminal victimisation have frequently been simplistic and unhelpful.

As Robert Elias (1990, 1993) has passionately argued, the victims' movement (if such it is – see Chapter Six) has largely been co-opted in the USA by conservative political parties and groups. The language of victim assistance has been used to justify harsher measures against offenders, including expensive and discriminatory 'wars' on drug misuse and particular types of crime. While legislation is passed to protect and assist victims, much of it goes unenforced. Funding previously available for the rehabilitation of offenders and the treatment of drug misusers is diverted into additional enforcement measures, which is unlikely to prove to be in the long-term interests of crime victims: 'In practice, offenders now have it worse, and yet we have done nothing to reduce the sources of their criminality' (Elias 1993, p.101).

There are strong parallels between this account of the American experience and what has been happening in Europe. Here, too, the New Right tries to make victims' issues part of the political campaign for 'law and order' – an attempt resolutely resisted by most European organisations representing victims themselves. As Phipps (1988) has pointed out, 'in a rather paradoxical way, victims in Conservative thinking are transformed from injured individuals into symbols of individual order' (p.180).

This makes it easier to understand why such a small proportion of the criminal justice budget under Conservative governments in the UK and elsewhere has been devoted to victim assistance, despite the political rhetoric about the need to support victims. Victims' needs have been the subject of lip-service, but have not received the degree of attention devoted to offenders. Cracking down on criminals was seen as the route to getting victims' votes, although this simplistic equation does not necessarily appeal to victims of crime very much.

Although we have not, in Europe, seen the kind of 'wars' on crime deplored by Elias, there is evidence of selective and discriminatory policing and sentencing (Dominelli et al. 1995; Smith 1995), and the political rhetoric of 'zero tolerance' and the appointment of a 'drugs czar' are reminiscent of American policies. People reporting rape, racial violence or harassment and domestic violence have a harder time getting their complaints taken seriously than people perceived as more 'deserving' victims (FitzGerald and Hale 1996; Lees 1997; Mullender 1996; see also Chapters Two and Four). Black people, in particular, are targeted for intensive policing operations and they are more likely than whites to be stopped and searched on the street, arrested and imprisoned (Cook and Hudson 1993; Dominelli *et al.* 1995).

We have few laws in the UK specifically aimed at protecting victims, but some of these do seem to go unenforced. For example, the provisions of the 1988 Criminal Justice Act are routinely ignored. Under this law, courts are required to give reasons when they fail to order compensation in cases where victims have sustained losses. In practice, this often does not happen (Moxon 1993). Similarly, the 1976 *Sexual Offences (Amendment) Act* makes it clear that the previous sexual history of witnesses in rape cases should be excluded from cross-examination unless the judge has reason to permit this type of questioning. Not only do judges frequently allow barristers to bring such issues up but defendants in rape cases are still protected from having their previous criminal convictions disclosed while the law allows the character of the women reporting rape to be impugned by barristers (Lees 1997).

Research in the Netherlands, similarly, shows that the 1988 legislation there, which requires the police and prosecution to keep victims informed of the progress of cases and of their rights to restitution, is poorly implemented. Only one-third of victims who seek information are kept informed and over 70 per cent of those suffering financial losses receive no compensation (Wemmers 1996). Furthermore, the police fail to refer victims needing help to the services set up to provide it (Wemmers and Zeilstra 1991). The failure to implement legislation and policies aimed at protecting and assisting victims is clearly not just a North American issue. Offender-orientated criminal justice systems find victims inherently difficult to accommodate and rhetorical commitments or symbolic adjustments are sometimes used as a substitute for real change (Weed 1995).

The final point in the summary of Elias' argument was that resources are diverted away from treatment and into punishment and enforcement. This has certainly been the case in the UK, where money has had to be found to finance a rapidly increasing prison population and a growing police service. Meanwhile, funding for Victim Support has been frozen and that for Women's Aid and Rape Crisis centres cut (Radford and Stanko 1991; Williams 1996a). Indeed, even the Criminal Injuries Compensation Scheme has been curtailed in the rush to cut costs (Koffman 1996; Victim Support 1996). It can safely be concluded that Elias' argument has some explanatory force in the European context.

The issue of politicisation is considered in greater detail in Chapter Four but it has been briefly examined here because of its importance in understanding some of the developments outlined in Chapter Two. In the next section the influence of academic studies of victimisation on popular views is examined.

Academic victimology and stereotypes of victims

Academic researchers in the social sciences often complain that their work is not used by practitioners or consulted when policies are drawn up. Occasionally, though, research findings (and the assumptions underlying them) achieve the status of common-sense knowledge. Once entrenched, such popular wisdom is difficult to challenge. Certain assumptions of a number of early studies of victims of crime have become embedded in the popular consciousness in this way.

It is difficult to know the extent to which early victimological researchers were responsible for *creating* stereotypes of victims: they may simply have expressed existing prejudices without giving them much thought. In either case, the repetition of stereotyped views of victims in academic literature gave such ideas increased legitimacy.

In 1948 Hans von Hentig published an influential study of crime victims which challenged the traditional criminological preoccupation with offenders. He argued, quite reasonably, that more attention should be given to victims and to the nature of their relationships with offenders. He believed that patterns were likely to emerge from such a study, which could be employed to prevent future victimisation. By classifying victims of crime in the ways he did, however, he contributed to the process of stereotyping. He wrote, for example, of an increased propensity to victimisation arising from 'mild depression... a disturbance of the instinct of self-preservation' (von Hentig 1967, p.420). The only evidence given is from other, equally anecdotal, studies. He goes on to argue that the victims of some sexual offences are themselves 'wanton' and to quote, with apparent approval, another author's view that 'a Negro will believe almost anything' and is, therefore, more likely to become the victim of confidence tricksters.

Of course, such examples, taken out of context, say more about the historical period in which they were written than they do about the subsequent development of victimology. What is important about von Hentig's work, however, is that it gave academic validation to his prejudices, and those of his contemporaries, about victims.

In the same tradition, Mendelsohn (1956) introduced the notion of victims' 'guilty contribution to the crime'. As Zedner (1997) points out,

Mendelsohn's continuum from 'completely innocent' to 'most guilty victim' was well-intended but its consequences remain with us today. Individualising victimisation in this way does not serve victims' interests at all well: once the study of victims began to concentrate on their relative culpability, it lost sight of the structural issues which lead to victimisation. The assessment of victims' guilt or innocence distracted attention from the causes of crime. It also reinforced a belief in the possibility of assessing the deservingness of individual victims. This justified (among other things) the restrictions on the payment of criminal injuries compensation to victims who happened to have a criminal record – the White Paper which proposed the creation of the compensation scheme specifically distinguished between 'innocent' and other victims (Home Office 1964; Koffman 1996).

Academic writing about rape has been particularly unhelpful until comparatively recently, feeding into patriarchal assumptions about 'victim-proneness' and even lending credence to offenders' claims that their victims encouraged them and participated willingly in their own brutalisation. Amir (1971), for example, argued that some rapes were 'victim precipitated'. He gave considerable prominence to offenders' accounts of what had occurred and drew his sample only from rapes recorded as such by the police. This led to methodological criticisms of his work and to feminist objections on the grounds that he was ideologically biased: his 'apparent endorsement of the common view that "nice girls" do not get raped... has been deemed most objectionable' (Zedner 1994, p.1210).

Amir's study was not an isolated aberration. Hindelang and colleagues published another book in the same tradition in 1978, which showed that victims who used force in response to threats or violence were likely to suffer greater injury themselves. This useful insight was taken by some observers (and practitioners such as police officers) to suggest that victims should remain passive in the face of threats and violence. Normandeau's study of robberies suggested that victims created what he called 'temptation-opportunity situations' (Normandeau 1968, p.110, cited in Walklate 1989). Similar studies were published in Poland. Bienek, for example, found that less than half of the rape victims interviewed were 'completely innocent' and that nearly 13 per cent of them were either careless or 'provocative'. According to Bienkowska, less than a quarter of the sample of women reporting rape had been assaulted involuntarily (Bienek 1974; Bienkowska 1984 – both in Polish, cited in Platek 1995).

Wolfgang (1958) went so far as to argue that more than a quarter of all murders were victim precipitated to a greater or lesser extent (based on an assessment of which of the parties first used or threatened violence). The idea of victim precipitation may have some explanatory power when examining ambiguous social encounters, such as assaults where the protagonists know each other. Analysing the degree of responsibility which can be attributed to the victim can seem like victim blaming, though, and it is difficult, in practice, to avoid giving this impression even if it is not intended. Fattah (1979) has suggested that it is possible to use explanatory concepts like 'victim-invited criminality' without necessarily getting into victim blaming, but it is hard to see how. Such approaches have done considerable damage in the past. As Walklate (1989) points out, they are not only objectionable because they let offenders off the hook and cause unnecessary suffering to victims but also because they neglect wider, structural causes of crime. The Freudian notion of the child as seducer, itself a version of victim precipitation theory, made it almost impossible for child sexual abuse to be effectively disclosed for many years, until an alternative theoretical framework became available (Walklate 1989). It is a short step, in practice, from seeking evidence of victim precipitation to blaming victims for their predicament.

The practical consequences of the victim blaming explicitly contained in some of these early victimological studies can be seen in the ways in which the police, courts, social workers and victim support agencies interact with victims. The assumption that a woman reporting rape has ulterior motives for doing so, and that the perpetrator's account is likely to be valid, actually prevents many women from going to the police. When cases do reach the courts, 'two opposing views are presented in rape trials and it is usually the woman's view that is discarded. The unreliability of the woman's word compared to the supposed rationality of men is a bias that judges express quite blatantly' (Lees 1997, p.68).

On a more mundane level, much crime-prevention policy is based upon an implicit form of victim blaming. Women are encouraged by the police to stay indoors, or at least to go out at night only when accompanied, on the assumption that they are responsible for taking sensible precautions to prevent their own victimisation. Why is it women, who commit few offences of violence, who are expected to vacate public spaces at dangerous times? Leaflets which advise women to change their lifestyles in order to avoid victimisation are a product of a discriminatory culture within the police forces which issue them, but there is some evidence that equal opportunities training and policies are having a progressive effect (Walklate 1996).

The 'common-sense' tendency to blame victims for their plight often works together with other powerful prejudices, such as sexist attitudes towards women, to disempower victims. While the trend towards self-blame may become part of the recovery process for some victims, in that it can be helpful for victims to identify and change behaviour which may have led to victimisation, they also need to accept that victimisation can simply occur at random.

Unfortunately, early victimological distinctions between the 'deserving' and 'undeserving' victim have lived on in modern thinking about victims of crime. An idealised image has emerged of the 'innocent' victim (as against the tarnished, blameworthy victims of sexual crimes, for example). As Walklate (1989) has shown, these idealisations are dangerous and need unpicking – they underlie much contemporary discussion of victims but are rarely made explicit or critically examined. No one need feel guilty about being targeted for victimisation and academic discourse which promotes such guilt is destructive and unnecessary. This is increasingly accepted among contemporary victimologists, but the common-sense distinctions between innocent and blameworthy victims live on in popular thinking and in professional practices.

Critical victimology

With the advent of feminist approaches to victimology, some of the long-standing assumptions of the discipline began to be questioned. Increasingly, from the 1970s, research studies appeared which challenged the idea of the male being treated as the norm in criminology in general (Carlen 1983; Heidensohn 1968; Smart 1977) and, specifically, in victimology (Dobash and Dobash 1979; Walklate 1989). A little later, a more generally critical victimology emerged, challenging the individualisation of issues relating to victims of crime and pointing out the relevance of structural causes (Christie 1993; Elias 1986; Fattah 1986; Mawby and Walklate 1994).

This new victimology has shown much more interest in the practical effects of theories and policies upon actual victims, and in the dynamic relationship between theorising and dealing with victims. It began by unpicking the assumptions beneath the individualistic, victim-blaming tradition (Miers 1989; Walklate 1989) but rapidly moved on to consider ways of improving services to victims and of altering traditional thinking about victims' rights (Mawby and Walklate 1994; Mullender 1996; Nettleton, Walklate and Williams 1997).

Rather than following the agenda dictated by powerful agencies such as government departments and police forces, these researchers have often gained access to individual victims and victim support projects at a local level (Hague, Malos and Dear 1996; Kosh and Williams 1995; Walklate 1984, 1986). Similarly, surveys of people's experiences of crime, often commissioned by local authorities, have concentrated upon gaining an understanding of victimisation in the context of the communities in which people live (Jones, MacLean and Young 1986; Kinsey 1984; Koffman 1996; Maguire and Bennett 1982; Walklate 1986). Such local crime surveys have revealed the unequal distribution of victimisation and have enquired into types of crime which the national survey fails to uncover (Maguire 1994). In particular, the prevalence of sexual and domestic violence has been revealed as much higher than previously assumed and it has been shown that people in certain areas are subject to very high levels of repeated victimisation. This applies not only to offences occurring in the context of a continuing relationship between victim and offender: there are inner-city districts where residents become accustomed to criminal victimisation, 'situations in which violence, abuse and petty theft are an integral part of victims' day-to-day existence' (Genn 1988, p.91).

This is of interest to local authorities for obvious reasons: not only are they concerned for the welfare of their citizens, but they also need to get crime under control if they are to attract inward investment, jobs and new residents. Information about crime rates and patterns was found to be useful in planning service provision. Surveys have, at times, been commissioned in response to concern about particular types of offence, as with racial harassment and violence (Saulsbury and Bowling 1991; Webster 1995). Central government has, at times, resisted local initiatives on crime – presumably in the belief that it should be dealt with at a national level. New Right social policy, while encouraging inter-agency partnerships at local level, tended to resist devolving power to local authorities. Crime prevention policies delivered at a local level, therefore, tend to be more developed under social democratic governments and to come under attack when conservative administrations take over. Thus, in the UK, the election of the new Labour government in 1997 was soon followed by proposals to make local authorities responsible for co-ordinating local crime-prevention strategies.

Changes of governing party have not, however, staunched the flow of local crime surveys and local victimological studies, which are now an important and established source of information.

A note on terminology

'Victims' or 'survivors'?

Not everyone who suffers victimisation likes to think of themselves as, or to be called, a victim. Feminists, including those involved with Rape Crisis centres, prefer to speak of survivors, for a number of reasons.

First, using the term 'survivor' makes clear the seriousness of rape as, often, a life-threatening attack. Second, public perceptions are shaped by terminology and the word 'victim' has connotations of passivity, even of helplessness. In the context of a movement which aims to empower people who have been victimised, this is clearly inappropriate: 'using the word "victim" to describe women takes away our power and contributes to the idea that it is right and natural for men to "prey" on us' (London Rape Crisis Centre 1984, p.ix).

Although the notion of survivors was introduced to counteract the negative implications of the term 'victim', there are dangers in treating the two concepts as if they were alternative identities. It is not particularly helpful to tell someone they are 'stuck' at the victim stage and should, therefore, move on to the survivor phase (see Kelly, Burton and Regan 1996; T. 1988). They may not be free to make such a choice and framing the issue in this way can lead people to feel that their way of coping is somehow inferior. Victims need positive reinforcement, including reassurance that their recovery is progressing, rather than the imposition of an ideal view of how their recovery should progress. Everyone develops their own coping mechanisms and it is inappropriately judgemental to try and force people to conform to some kind of typology.

In this book the word 'victim' is used of all who have been criminally victimised, with the exception of the offences of murder and rape. Frequent reference is made to the survivors of murder victims for the obvious reason that the direct victim of the offence is dead. In this context the term 'survivor' carries more than its literal meaning: for reasons which are explained in Chapter Three, the people bereaved by a murder experience extreme suffering and need considerable support. In deference to feminist arguments about the inappropriateness of using the word 'victim' to describe people who have been raped, reference is made to 'survivors', except where victims of a number of types of offence, including rape, are described.

Victim Support and victim support

When discussing the national UK umbrella organisation, reference will be made to Victim Support with capitals. At other times the phrase victim support (or victim support agencies) will be used to denote the whole range of sources of support for victims of crime. It is usually obvious from the context which meaning is intended, but readers may find it useful to have the distinction pointed out at this stage.

'Domestic' violence

Although its use is well established, the term 'domestic violence' has unfortunate and misleading connotations. The domestic nature of the violence makes it sound almost homely and the phrase plays down 'both the social and the gendered dimensions of the problem' (Whalen 1996, p.18). Where it is used, for convenience, in what follows, inverted commas are employed to remind the reader of the problematic, if convenient, nature of the term.

Women's Aid

In the UK the refuge movement has been known, since the 1970s, as Women's Aid, although the umbrella body co-ordinating this work is now known as Refuge. Refuges are called shelters in North America. For the sake of clarity, the term 'Women's Aid' is used throughout the book to refer to the refuge movement.

A methodological note

A range of sources has been drawn upon in the process of writing this book. Where the work of others is quoted or summarised, conventional references are given. Quotations which are not followed by a reference are from the transcripts of interviews undertaken specifically for the book, which, for reasons which will become obvious, are mostly anonymous. Both group and individual interviews were conducted, depending upon the nature of the agency, and informants were offered the opportunity to check a transcript. These have been used in the construction of case studies as well as being occasionally quoted directly. Three group and five individual interviews were conducted with representatives of a variety of agencies, as well as numerous enquiries by letter, email and telephone.

CHAPTER TWO

Repeated Criminal Victimisation

This chapter examines the phenomenon of repeated criminal victimisation and looks at why some people are victimised over and over again while others seem to escape altogether. It then goes on to consider the impact of factors such as race, gender, age, disability and class upon rates of victimisation, and the relationship between membership of various vulnerable groups and the fear of crime. Finally, the characteristics of offenders are briefly examined in the light of knowledge about the factors which predispose people to becoming their victims.

Repeated victimisation

Some people become victims of crime, not once but repeatedly. Early research on victims examined the phenomenon of repeat victimisation and there was a tendency in some of this work to blame victims themselves for their predicament, or at least to appear to do so (see Chapter One). More recent researchers have argued that linking repeat victimisation to the victims' lifestyle or behaviour diverts attention away from broader issues like class and gender divisions, and thereby individualises the social processes by which victims are created (Genn 1988; Morris 1987; Walklate 1989). Relating this insight to specific types of offence makes it obvious that repeat victimisation is more complex than simply being a matter of lifestyle or of victims somehow provoking offending: violence against women in the home, or the sexual abuse of children, or racially-motivated assaults, occur in a particular social context of structured inequality. How the victim behaves may have little or no influence on whether victimisation recurs.

While there is clearly a need to identify characteristics and behaviour which might make people more vulnerable to victimisation, it is unhelpful to make individual victims feel guilty about being offended against, for several reasons. First, because such feelings are likely to hinder their recovery and make it less likely that they will receive appropriate help. Second, if people feel guilty about being victimised, they are less likely to report offences, which increases the danger that others will be victimised by the same offender. Also, from a public policy point of view, it is unwise to create conditions which make it easier for frequent offenders to go undetected and it is, therefore, undesirable to stigmatise people who are repeatedly victimised. The concept of 'vulnerability' to victimisation also needs to be used with care: people have many other statuses as well as that of victim of crime and there is a danger, on the one hand, of over-simplifying the issue and, on the other, of appearing to patronise victims. Some victims are vulnerable because they belong to particular groups; others, however, are victimised because they are young and aggressive and go to crime-prone areas looking for trouble (see Newburn and Stanko 1994a).

Repeated victimisation is very common, as anyone involved in work with crime victims knows. Indeed, analysis of the 1992 British Crime Survey suggested that 4.3 per cent of victims were chronically victimised, suffering five or more crimes over the period of a single year. This small group of victims suffered 43.5 per cent of all reported crime (Farrell and Pease 1993). Forty per cent of all house burglaries affect 3 or 4 per cent of households (Pease 1997). The problem is compounded by the concentration of such chronic victimisation among members of groups already disadvantaged for other reasons – they tend to live in poor areas, among high concentrations of offenders and many are black (Genn 1988).

Although it took a long time for the relevant agencies to react to such statistics (which have been available since the 1970s),[1] the police have reorganised their responses to repeated victimisation in recent years. At first, it was difficult (because of the ways in which crime statistics were recorded) to identify repeated offences against a particular victim or property. There was also an understandable reticence about telling people who had just been victimised that a repeated offence was statistically likely: 'there might be an emotional reluctance to be frank about it because it may evoke fear of crime. It is not reassuring to tell a victim that a burglar may indeed come back' (Farrell and Pease 1993, p.3).

---

[1]   Bridgeman and Sampson (1994) cite a series of studies dated 1973–81. The most influential was probably Sparks, Genn and Dodd (1977).

Police officers are now encouraged to look for patterns of repeat victimisation when called to the scene of a crime and the computerised recording system has been altered to make it easier to make such connections. Once repeated victimisation is identified, a range of agencies can be mobilised to make a co-ordinated response – 'For example, a successful domestic burglary prevention project in Rochdale included a combination of upgrading household security, property marking, "cocoon" neighbourhood watch and offender programmes' (Bridgeman and Sampson 1994, p.9; see also Forrester *et al.* 1990).

Bridgeman and Sampson's study was primarily concerned with crime prevention, which is probably why it emphasised these predominantly practical measures. The argument can be extended, however. As well as receiving priority from the police and other agencies involved in crime prevention, people who are repeatedly victimised can also be targeted by those offering emotional support. This already happens to some extent but the voluntary agencies supporting victims may need to consider marshalling their own resources more effectively in their work with the revictimised.

Case study

Mark Wilson is referred to the local Victim Support scheme by the police after being attacked by a group of three white youths on leaving a town-centre pub. He has cuts and bruises to his face, damage to one eye and a broken bone in his hand. Although the attack was over quickly, it has had a severe impact: Mark is reluctant to leave home and has been off work for several days. When Victim Support volunteer Joe Brown phones him, the conversation lasts twenty minutes and Joe concludes by arranging to visit him.

Mark is quite clear that he was attacked purely because he is black. The youths made racist remarks before and during the assault. Although he had given full descriptions of two of the attackers, the police seemed to feel that it would be difficult to trace them. He was particularly upset about the attack because he had been involved in another, less serious, incident the previous week when he had been jostled and slapped in the same pub by a group of young men, one of whom was at school with him, and then asked to leave by the landlord, along with his assailants.

After a long discussion, Joe suggests that Mark explains to his employer why he has not felt able to return to work. They rehearse the telephone conversation. Although the previous incident was not reported to the police, the close proximity of the two events has sapped

Mark's confidence. Joe tells him about the local Racial Harassment Project and agrees to ring him with its phone number. Before leaving, he arranges to call again the following week.

The second time they meet, Mark is feeling better and has made an appointment with a worker at the Racial Harassment Project. He has also decided to contact the man he remembers from the assault in the pub and tell him how he felt about that incident. If he is not satisfied with the response, he will complain to the pub landlord. Meanwhile, Joe has spoken to the Victim Support co-ordinator, who recalls another case of racial harassment in the same pub, and it is agreed that this will be taken up with the police inspector who sits on the Victim Support scheme's committee in the hope that this will result in police action. Mark says he will also mention it to the Racial Harassment project worker with a view to considering making a complaint to the licensing magistrates.

This case study shows that victims can be empowered if they are encouraged to deal with the aftermath of offending. Without taking the law into his own hands, Mark is enabled to take steps to put the incidents behind him and do something about both the offenders and the venue where the attacks occurred. Joe listens and gives information, advice and support, leaving it to Mark to take most of the action. While victims appreciate the neighbourly gesture involved in contacting them after an offence, they often want to do things themselves and many do not require a visit from Victim Support at all. In some cases a specialist agency is able to provide appropriate support, often in collaboration with other local services such as housing departments and police. The volunteer can use specialist knowledge to facilitate this process while leaving the ownership of the problem in the victim's hands.

Victimisation and gender, race, class and disability

Common sense suggests that certain types of offence have particular kinds of victims. For example, it is reasonable to assume that racial harassment primarily affects members of ethnic minority groups and that 'domestic' violence is mainly perpetrated against women. Even these apparently obvious links are not entirely straightforward, however, and caution needs to be exercised when making such assumptions. The categories involved are socially constructed and subject to change – for example, it was axiomatic until comparatively recently that rape was, by definition, an offence with a female victim. Changes to the law in a number of countries now make it essential to differentiate between rapes committed against women and men. The creation of a new offence arose from a questioning of the legal definitions by victims and others: lived experience did not bear out the existing definition of rape. Once victims are given the chance to speak for themselves, they tend to question some of the categories in which they have traditionally been placed.

When young people were asked open-ended questions about their experience of various types of crime in Keighley, West Yorkshire, they reported high levels of racial abuse and violence. Not only the Asian respondents but also the white youths said that they had experienced such incidents. On further examination, it appeared that Asian young people saw themselves as resisting the effects of racial hostility and aggression by 'standing their ground' and defending particular pieces of territory against white 'intruders' (Webster 1995). Thus white members of this age group were being drawn, against their wishes in many cases, into racial disputes. This example shows that even such a seemingly straightforward category as racial harassment can reveal considerable complexity on closer scrutiny.

A further complication soon becomes obvious if one attempts to generalise about the likelihood of members of particular social groups being criminally victimised. Most victims are likely to belong to more than one of the groups under examination. Thus it is often impossible to tell whether black people are over-represented among the victims of a particular type of crime because they are black, or because they live in a particular area, or are also poor or female, or simply because the sample contained a large proportion of black people. Many victims will fall into several 'vulnerable' categories. Generalisations of this kind should, therefore, be made cautiously, if at all, and such generalisations should be viewed with scepticism.

This need not deter us, however, from trying to understand some of the evidence that there are meaningful patterns in the statistics on criminal victimisation. The figures do have something useful to say about the comparative propensity of members of racial minorities, women, young people, older people and those with disabilities to become victims of crime. The disproportionate likelihood of members of particular disadvantaged groups suffering specific types of victimisation is also clearly of interest.

Before embarking on an examination of the evidence for these assertions, a note of caution is necessary. Crime itself is socially defined and certain types of behaviour, while subject to criminal sanctions, are less likely than others to be reported, processed and dealt with as crimes. This issue is discussed at some length in the literature on 'critical victimology' (see, for example, Elias 1993, 1994; Mawby and Walklate 1994; McShane and Williams 1992).

Two particular aspects of the discussion relate directly to questions about the susceptibility of members of certain social groups to be victimised: certain criminal behaviour is unlikely to be treated as such in many cases and victims in some circumstances are reluctant to take formal legal action.

First, some types of behaviour, although definable as criminal, are rarely dealt with as such. Some of the critical victimologists have suggested that the 'crimes of the powerful' are far more significant than the offences dealt with by the formal criminal justice system because they have many more victims. Elias (1994), for example, argues that 'corporations produce extensive harms, and far more victimization – measured in terms of injuries, deaths, and financial losses – than common crimes' (p.18).

Walklate (1989) gives a number of examples of what she calls 'corporate victimization', where people died as a result of negligence. She suggests that there may well have been criminal negligence involved in the deaths of large numbers of workers on North Sea oil platforms (including those killed in the Piper Alpha accident) and in the production and sale of thalidomide, the drug which caused birth defects in 8000 children around the world. These events were recast by the media as 'disasters' for which no one was to blame and the corporate perpetrators were never arraigned. In such cases victims struggle to be recognised as such and compensation can take years to obtain through the civil (rather than the criminal) courts (Box 1983; Mawby and Walklate 1994). Slapper (1994) makes a similar argument in respect of the Herald of Free Enterprise ferry disaster, in which 192 people died as a result of negligence but the operators were not prosecuted.

Corporate crime may well impact more severely upon members of already disadvantaged groups than on people with access to the resources required to pursue the companies concerned through the courts. The parents of children affected by thalidomide were assisted in their campaign by investigative journalists and might not otherwise have been able to obtain compensation. The low-paid workers of multinational corporations in Third World countries are generally unlikely to be able to pursue claims for criminal negligence against firms which allow them to be poisoned at work (as at Bhopal in 1984 – see Pearce and Tombs 1993). On a smaller scale, two-thirds of fatal accidents at work in England and Wales involve violations of the Health and Safety at Work Act, which provides for criminal prosecution of managers who are proved to be at fault. Yet less than 40 per cent of workplace deaths lead to the prosecution of an employer (Croall 1992).

Quite apart from corporate and white collar crime, there are other categories of illegal behaviour which are comparatively unlikely to result in prosecution and these also seem likely to affect members of already vulnerable groups disproportionately. So-called 'domestic' violence often occurs repeatedly over a long period of time but only specimen offences are prosecuted and the great majority of such violence probably goes unreported. This makes it difficult to know how prevalent this type of behaviour is and even victim surveys probably underestimate its incidence because of respondents' fear and embarrassment. Police responses, and prosecution service policies, may also represent forms of screening, preventing many offences from going to court (Cretney and Davis 1995). There is some evidence that victims who have had a longer education are more likely to report such offences, which suggests that working-class women are generally less likely to prosecute their assailants (Walklate 1989). These factors combine to make victimisation statistics very misleading.

This links with the second special factor relating to the victimisation of members of oppressed groups: criminal behaviour may represent part of that process of oppression, making victims reluctant to report it. They may feel that the police, courts and other authorities represent part of the problem, rather than offering a solution. Webster (1995), for example, notes that Asian young people hesitate to report racial harassment to the police because they do not trust them. In many cases this is because their previous contact has been in the role of suspects (and it is notoriously difficult to differentiate between assailants and victims in cases of assault and affray). Where relations between police and victims improve, reporting rates increase, making it appear that more offences are occurring (see Jenness 1995; Pease 1997).

Another factor, which applies both to racial harassment and to 'domestic' violence, is the increased level of tolerance built up by people for whom victimisation is very frequent. They do not report each individual incident because some come to stand out as more serious than others and because to report each occurrence would involve them in constant contact with the authorities: 'For some sections of the community criminal victimization is a way of life; it is part of their everyday existence' (Walklate 1989, p.155).

An additional factor for some victims of racial harassment and assaults is the language barrier: if the police, housing departments and other agencies to which victims might report crime do not make use of interpreters, some offences are unlikely to come to their attention for that reason (Sampson and Phillips 1995).

This not only distorts the statistics but also means that those studying the issue are in danger of forgetting that there are sectors of the population for whom victimisation is so frequent that it does not seem out of the ordinary to them. Society is increasingly stratified according to the extent to which people have to face various kinds of risk (Beck 1992; Parton 1996) and there are geographical areas where the risk of criminal victimisation is indeed an everyday consideration. In such areas, and in the families where 'domestic' violence is routine, the solutions offered by the criminal justice system may begin to seem irrelevant. This raises questions about the purpose and usefulness of studying victims in isolation from the larger social forces which victimise them – issues considered in Chapter Four.

In the remainder of this chapter some of the factors linking members of oppressed and vulnerable groups to particular types of criminal victimisation are briefly outlined. A pattern emerges of crime as part of the process of oppression of members of particular groups and of crime against people because their vulnerability makes them softer targets. This is discussed further at the end of the chapter.

Race and victimisation

It is difficult to disentangle the effects of race and other factors upon the high levels of criminal victimisation experienced by black people, but it is important to hear what black crime victims themselves say about that experience. Because black people are more likely than white people to live in areas with high crime rates, to be unemployed and to have lower incomes, they are susceptible to victimisation for these reasons as well as because of their race. It is, therefore, hardly surprising that their overall victimisation rates are higher than those for white people, although in England and Wales the difference is largely accounted for (at least in respect of most offences) by variables other than race (Mawby and Walklate 1994).

The literature suggests that black people 'attribute racial motivation to many of the crimes they experience', particularly in the case of offences of violence and vandalism (Mayhew, Elliott and Dowds 1989, p.46; Mayhew, Aye Maung and Mirrlees-Black 1993). When asked why they viewed the crimes in this way, 70 per cent of black victims reported that the offender used racist language (Mayhew, Aye Maung and Mirrlees-Black 1993).[2] One

2   In view of this clear evidence of racial motivation, the researchers' reluctance to take informants at their word seems rather over-cautious, although it is conceivable that

factor discouraging people from reporting racial abuse and violence was the experience of not being taken seriously when reporting previous similar incidents, although this can change if it is made clear that the local authorities are taking a proactive approach (Sampson and Phillips 1995). Until the findings of such research are more widely taken up, dissatisfaction with the criminal justice system and its treatment of victims of racist crime are likely to remain at high levels among black people (MacLeod, Prescott and Carson 1996).

Reporting a crime and being ignored is likely to be particularly annoying when the incident is seen as in some way shameful, and many victims of racist crime do see it as such. As a Bengali man told researchers in London: '[I] feel ashamed and degraded repeatedly reporting incidents. That is why I sometimes do not report' (Sampson and Phillips 1995, p.16). Other victims described their homes as prisons, and one shopkeeper said: 'Racial incidents have been happening for the last four years. I don't call it my shop I call it my torture chamber... the only way to change this problem is to change my colour... There is a limit to how much abuse anyone can take' (Sampson and Phillips 1995, p.14).

So the emotional impact of crime, and particularly of this kind of hate crime,[3] has to be taken into account as well as its seriousness and frequency. There is plenty of evidence that black people are among those most profoundly affected by victimisation (Jones, MacLean and Young 1986; Sampson and Phillips 1995; Walklate 1989). Given the combination of being victimised and the racist intent of the perpetrators, racially-motivated crime is obviously very hurtful: 'a racist incident is about the misuse of power; the collective power enjoyed by white people in a society structured by racist ideologies and discriminatory practices' (Troyna and Hatcher 1992, p.495).

offenders are more likely to hold racist views than non-offenders and to express them when coincidentally confronted with black victims. The distinction between 'racial' and racist incidents is an important one, not always made by writers in this area. Crime committed as a result of racial hatred, or as part of a pattern of racial oppression, needs to be distinguished from coincidentally inter-racial offences (Troyna and Hatcher 1992).

3   'Hate crime' refers to offences motivated by hatred of members (or people perceived as members) of particular groups, including racial hatred, homophobia, sexism, ageism and disablism. The term is enshrined in legislation in the USA and Canada. The American legislation requires hate crime rates to be officially monitored (see Jenness 1995 and Chapter Six).

So far, the discussion has concentrated upon personal crime, such as violence, threats, robbery and vandalism.[4] Not all inter-racial crime is motivated by racial hatred, however, and the relationship between race and other factors needs to be considered. Racist incidents would probably account for a large proportion of assaults upon black people (who are, on average, almost twice as likely as other people to be victims of assault (Jones, MacLean and Young 1986) and for whom such offences are often part of a pattern of repeated abuse). Racism does not, however, directly explain the high rate of car thefts suffered by Afro-Caribbean and Asian victims, or the propensity of both groups to suffer thefts involving no offender-victim contact (Mayhew, Elliott and Dowds 1989). In these cases the combination of other factors affecting black people disproportionately (including low income, unemployment and living in inner-city areas) helps to account for their over-representation in the figures.

It is clear that black people are, for a variety of reasons, likely to suffer higher rates of crime than white people. Some of the steps being taken by criminal justice and voluntary agencies to redress this balance, and some of the additional work that needs to be done, are considered in Chapters Five and Six.

Gender and victimisation

According to criminal statistics, women in England and Wales have a relatively low risk of suffering most types of crime, but crime surveys show that it generally has a greater impact on them than similar offences have upon men (perhaps because women are more likely to be the victims of violent crime by known offenders, which are more emotive in nature) (Mawby and Walklate 1994). These headline figures, however, conceal large disparities between female and male victimisation rates in relation to particular types of offence, and they do not reflect the extent of unreported 'domestic' violence against women.

The Islington Crime Survey, for example, which was one of the first such surveys to use methods capable of uncovering incidents of 'domestic' violence, found higher rates of female victimisation than previous research and

---

4   The different types of offence affect different racial groups differentially. Asians are at particular risk of vandalism and threats, while Afro-Caribbeans have a high risk of assault, including 'domestic' violence, and burglary. Both groups have a higher risk of street robbery and theft from the person than white people.

much greater risk from violent offences than the official crime statistics suggested (Walklate 1989). In particular, women were 'half as likely again as men to be assaulted' (Jones, MacLean and Young 1986, p.65). This is clearly very significant and, although it raises important issues in relation to survey methodology, also draws attention to larger questions. While anyone may become a victim of crime, members of some groups are more at risk than others – and these include not only 'minority' groups but, where personal violence is concerned, also women (who form a majority of the population). This has substantial political implications, which are discussed in Chapter Four.

Women decide not to report violence within domestic relationships for a variety of reasons. One was mentioned in connection with racist violence: people feel ashamed and guilty about being victimised, not least because of the continuing assumption that women 'ask for it' (Stanko 1988). This is compounded by police responses to such offences when they are reported: even though, in response to feminist campaigning, police forces now as a matter of policy take violence within the home more seriously, individual officers have not necessarily changed their views.[5] Local inter-agency agreements can alter the climate, which, in turn, leads to a higher reporting rate. Local community safety units are increasingly applying research findings on such inter-agency work to their own areas (see George 1998 on the Domestic Violence Intervention Project in Hammersmith and Fulham, London).

Similarly, the police have improved their response to rape victims, but not as much as many commentators feel they need to (Lees 1996; Temkin 1996, 1997; Walklate 1996). Meanwhile, the judicial system continues to revictimise many complainants in rape cases (Lees 1996, 1997). Women who have suffered the consequences of reporting an offence which was not taken seriously will not quickly do so again.[6] Women who do report violent attacks frequently decide not to press charges because of fear of the assailant, and

---

5   Reporting rates increased throughout the 1980s, suggesting that women are becoming more willing to report assaults (Levi 1994).

6   Lees (1996) notes that, despite improvements in forensic tests, the number of rape convictions in England and Wales remained static during a period when the number of rapes reported more than doubled (1985–1993 statistics). Cretney and Davis (1995) point out that 'domestic' assault perpetrators are normally bailed when an offence is reported to the police and are likely to be fined rather than dealt with more severely in most cases. This varies from place to place.

even serious assaults are often not prosecuted in such circumstances (Cretney and Davis 1995).

Although crime surveys do uncover some unreported crime, victims whose attacker is with them at the time of the interview are hardly likely to disclose their experience of violence in the home to a researcher. Such surveys normally also concentrate on discrete incidents rather than on processes and, as such, they are not a good way of finding out about repeated victimisation by the same perpetrator over a period of time (Genn 1988).

If, as feminist research using in-depth interviewing has shown, as many as one in five women have been raped at some time in their lives, it is hardly surprising that women fear crime more than men (Stanko 1988). Other research has confirmed high levels of actual and threatened violence against women, with more than half the respondents having experienced threat, violence or sexual harassment within the previous year (Maguire 1994). The fear of such crime, and the criminal justice system's failure to protect victims, help to sustain patriarchy (see Radford and Stanko 1991, and Chapter Four).

The relationship between gender and criminal victimisation is a complex one. It is important to remember that some men will find it difficult to recover from victimisation and that some forms of offending against men cause particular fear and insecurity which is not readily acknowledged at present. Newburn and Stanko (1994a) give the examples of offences of violence and sexual assaults: many men fear violence and male victims of sexual assaults are faced with having to adjust their view of their own masculinity and their vulnerability. The present tendency to give a low priority to the emotional needs of young male victims of violence is probably mistaken. While they may, in some cases, contribute to their own victimisation, this does not necessarily make it any less painful for them (Maguire and Corbett 1987).

Men and women may be targeted for violence and abuse because of their sexuality. While hate crimes of this kind are recognised in American law, homophobia is no more than an aggravating factor in deciding upon sentences in assault cases in other countries – and the failure to recognise hatred of lesbians and gay men as a cause of violence means that many cases go unreported. The rise of victim assistance programmes and associated public awareness campaigns has increased the visibility of this kind of crime in the USA, building upon the earlier success of the women's movement in demanding appropriate responses to male violence against women, but official agencies continue to under-record it there due to prejudice or lack of awareness among their own personnel (Jenness 1995; see also Chapter Six).

Disability and victimisation

With the exception of the sexual abuse of people with learning difficulties, there has, until recently, been very little research interest in the incidence of crime against people with disabilities, although there is clear evidence that people who are vulnerable for whatever reason are more likely to become victims of crime. Most of the available research evidence is from North America.

Crime surveys explicitly exclude people living in institutional care, although this is one of the highest risk settings for sexual offences against people with disabilities. Such surveys also fail to ask people interviewed in the community whether they are disabled, despite the high rate of public order and sexual offending against people with learning difficulties (Carmody 1991; Sanders et al. 1997; Sobsey 1994; Williams 1995). When one project for sexual assault survivors in Australia began to monitor the proportion of referrals which related to people with disabilities, it rapidly became clear that a disproportionate number of the survivors were 'intellectually disabled' and that the majority of the perpetrators were 'personnel working with clients, family members, fellow residents or employees' (Carmody 1991, p.230). It may be that people with physical disabilities are particularly vulnerable to victimisation in the home, but official information is simply not available. They are certainly at much greater risk of sexual victimisation if they are in institutional care, particularly from care staff (Sobsey 1994).

The police sometimes do not take complaints by people with learning difficulties seriously. Even where offences are reported to the police and proceeded with, prosecutions are often dropped because the prosecuting authority takes the view that witnesses with learning difficulties are incapable of giving credible evidence (although in many cases they have already been able to give coherent statements to police). Such decisions are usually made by people who have not met the complainant in the case. As a result, offences go unreported and the free movement of people with disabilities is constrained by fear of crime. In Canada the federal criminal code has been amended to create specific offences of exploitation of people with disabilities and to ensure that disabled people have equal access to the criminal justice system (Philpot 1997). A campaign by *Community Care* magazine has put this matter on the political agenda and the treatment of defendants and witnesses with learning difficulties is being reviewed as part of a wider inter-departmental review of the criminal justice system (*Community Care* 1998).

The failure to deal satisfactorily with minor crime may lead victims to tolerate quite serious abuse without formal complaints being made: they become accustomed to abusive behaviour and poor policing practice (Luckasson 1992; Sanders *et al.* 1997; Williams 1995). Many disabled victims of sexual abuse and assault lack faith in the criminal justice system as a result of previous experience, and so decide not to report offences, which may become 'a self-fulfilling prophecy, as crimes that go unreported cannot be punished' (Sobsey 1994, p.79). Furthermore, the well-founded fear of victimisation often damages the social lives of people with disabilities, even discouraging them from leaving institutions, if they are aware of acquaintances who have been victimised in the community and not had their complaints taken seriously (Luckasson 1992).

Everyone coming into contact with people with learning disabilities needs training on the law and learning difficulties, and on how to protect victims with disabilities and avoid collusion with offenders. Williams (1995) has provided specimen training materials. The use of euphemisms such as 'neglect' or 'discrimination' when discussing what are essentially hate crimes such as assaults, abuse and vandalism directed at people with disabilities does nothing to clarify the issues (Luckasson 1992) and such training should explore this. The particular vulnerability of people with disabilities to sexual and financial exploitation needs to be highlighted in staff training and recognised in policies designed to protect users of social services. Interestingly, the American legislation on hate crimes does not apply to victims with disabilities: 'The law does seek to protect disabled people, but only when they can be construed as vulnerable and lacking a choice about leaving the violent situation' (Waxman 1991, p.190).

The criminal justice system has gone much further in some provinces of Canada, making special provision for all witnesses (and for jurors and defendants) with any kind of communication difficulties (Philpot 1997).

Courses aimed at improving care workers' awareness of attitudes to disability can usefully explore the psychological and political factors which underlie the distinction commonly made between, for example, violence motivated by anti-Semitism or racism, on the one hand, and hate crime against people with disabilities on the other. Carmody (1991) noted that potential victims also have a need for 'training': 'A lack of sex education and opportunities to develop a sexual identity results in confusion, and uncertainty about what is acceptable behaviour from other people' (p.231).

Where victims do not receive counselling or support at the time of an offence, this stores up problems for the future, as they are then likely to need longer-term treatment when they do disclose their abuse (Carmody 1991) and perpetrators are more likely to reoffend against them or offend against others.

People with disabilities are, in all probability, more likely than the non-disabled to be the victims of offences of dishonesty and deception (Sanders et al. 1997; Sobsey 1994), but, again, the evidence is hard to come by. In California specialist police units have been set up to assist the victims of financial abuse, including rich, elderly, retired film stars. In many parts of North America there are Adult Protective Teams which bring together the relevant professionals to work with victims of elder abuse. At a hospital in St. Vincent, Ohio, for example, the team includes social workers, doctors and nurses, a dietitian, a legal advisor and the chaplaincy. Its members can liaise with community agencies, including courts and the police, in cases where financial exploitation of patients is suspected.

These arrangements are modelled upon child protection teams (Parkins 1996), which may not be the best model to take. The Law Commission in England, considering stronger legal protection for vulnerable older people, also made proposals based upon inter-agency child protection work and it was pointed out that there are intrinsic social and legal differences between children and adults which this failed to take into account (Brammer 1996). There is a danger that conceptualising fraud and theft from older people as elder abuse belittles the seriousness of such offences and leads effectively to decriminalisation (Hugman 1994), as with child abuse in the early days of interdisciplinary work. However, the American example shows that financial abuse can be dealt with effectively using such an approach.

Disabled victims are often implicitly blamed for their predicament, when assumptions are made about assaults and other abuse being precipitated by the stress experienced by their carers. As Sobsey (1994) has pointed out, this is a subtle variation on the old theme of victim blaming (see Chapter One). The idea that disabled people bring abuse and exploitation on themselves springs from a medical or 'deficit' model of disability which emphasises people's physical or psychological impairments and neglects to consider the social and environmental constraints which limit their potential. The medical model also avoids any consideration of the power relations involved in crime against people with disabilities (Shakespeare 1996). Only when disability is considered in social terms does it become apparent that it is socially constructed: the barriers put in place by the non-disabled are the real limitations on the opportunities available to people with disabilities, rather than their physical or mental impairment.

People with disabilities are particularly vulnerable to a variety of forms of abuse and crime for a number of reasons. Among these is the contempt towards disabled people felt by many of the non-disabled. Manifestations of this include what Tom Shakespeare (1996) calls 'justification' of sexual abuse. He notes that sexual abusers of people with disabilities sometimes excuse and attempt to justify their behaviour by arguing that the victims were sexually unattractive and would not have the opportunity of engaging in sexual activity in any other context. The abuse is justified on the basis of the argument that the abuser is somehow doing the victim a favour. He goes on to say:

> There is a wider justification for abuse of disabled people, in terms of the fear and hatred that nondisabled society has for disabled people. There is a tendency to hate those who are perceived as weak; to oppress those who are threatening; to pick on the underdog. I think those without social power or those who are insecure prey on other people who they perceive as inferior to them, and replicate their powerlessness and hurt on these lesser victims. (p.208)

Waxman (1991) offers a number of other explanations, including cultural stereotypes of disability which justify social exclusion and violence. The media frequently portray villains as disabled people and this is a long tradition which goes back to William Shakespeare and, further, to Greek myth. She points out that 'Violence also masquerades as medical treatment with such practices as institutionalization, electro-convulsive therapy, eugenic sterilization, medical experimentation' (p.189).

She goes on to argue that there are deep-seated psychological reasons for the dislike and disgust aroused by disability. If we believe that acquired disability inevitably involves social isolation, the loss of control over one's life, indeed 'the loss of an essential part of one's humanity' (p.193), we may shun people with disabilities to avoid being reminded that this could happen to anyone, including ourselves. Displaying and expressing pity towards people with disabilities, and characterising them as bravely coping with tragedy, allows us to express our contempt in an apparently benign manner. These patronising attitudes mask assumptions of superiority over disabled people.

The criminal justice system has been slow to adapt its procedures in recognition of the particular vulnerability of some people with disabilities. In some parts of Canada there is a statutory requirement that professional people must report any cases of suspected abuse or crime against disabled service users. Although this can create other problems (for example, when victims do not want the matter pursued through the courts) it makes social expectations clear (Roeher Institute 1995). In Australia victims and witnesses with learning disabilities have a legal right to bring a supporter with them to court and into the witness box (Sanders *et al.* 1997). In Canada this extends to jury service: regulations have been specifically amended to allow more than twelve people into the jury room if jurors need signers or interpreters (Philpot 1997). In the UK the question of whether a supporter can accompany a witness is currently at the judge's discretion, although it has recently been decided that such issues will be settled prior to trials and, if cases are adjourned, judges new to the case will no longer be able to reverse previous decisions.

What is needed is a recognition that different kinds of participants in the criminal justice process need different types of support and preparation before and while attending the court. The idea that counselling for victims, to help them deal with the effects of offences, must wait until after the accused has been tried is extraordinarily inhumane. It confuses counselling with the coaching of witnesses, when the two can easily be distinguished in practice (Sanders *et al.* 1997). The system needs to recognise that 'normal procedures which create formal equality between defendant and victim often create substantive inequality when the victim is vulnerable' (Sanders *et al.* 1997, pp.86–7).

There are many types of vulnerability and police officers should be trained to recognise them and respond appropriately, as should social workers, probation officers, court clerks, ushers, judges and lawyers.

Age and victimisation

People may be seen as vulnerable because they are young or because they are old. The extent of criminal victimisation is higher among both age groups, but the reasons are different and they will, therefore, be considered separately.

Older victims

As with other characteristics which make people vulnerable to victimisation, it is difficult to disentangle the age factor from others which mean that older people figure prominently among those for whom victimisation has a high impact. In terms of actual rates of victimisation, older people are at relatively low risk from crime (although elder abuse, which is not considered here as such, is certainly under-reported[7]) (Mawby and Walklate 1994): 'victimization patterns are not necessarily age specific but are related to factors which are more common in the elderly such as poverty, dependency and social isolation' (Schwarz 1991, p.73)

Perhaps because they are often vulnerable in other ways,[8] older victims tend to report that crime has a high and long-lasting impact upon them compared to younger victims. Surprisingly little attention has been paid by researchers in recent years to the victimisation of elderly people. While they may be relatively unlikely to become victims of crime, their fears are understandable: if they are poor, in poor health or isolated, or if they feel vulnerable, their ability to withstand victimisation may be substantially reduced (Zedner 1997).

There has been a tendency for politicians to talk airily of fear of crime being a greater problem than crime itself and to point out the contradiction between the facts that older people – particularly women – are at the lowest risk of personal crime but that they are among the most likely to avoid going out at night due to their fear of being victimised.

Criticising people's fears as irrational does not make them feel any safer! (See Crawford *et al.* 1990; Hanmer and Stanko 1985; Young 1988.) Indeed, victimisation rates may actually be as low as they are due to women and older people avoiding going out at night because they do not feel safe doing so (Young 1994). Fattah and Sacco (1989) conclude their careful study of crime against older people in North America with the following comments, which remain relevant today:

---

7   For further information on elder abuse see Fattah and Sacco (1989); Pritchard (1992); Kingston and Penhale (1995). The border between elder abuse and crime is a blurred one and it commonly takes the form of financial exploitation (Blunt 1993).

8   For example, in the case of financial abuse of people who are elderly and disabled or confused, and in the case of assaults upon the frail elderly or those who are dependent upon their assailant for essential daily care.

While it may be fashionable to view fear of crime as an irrational response on the part of the elderly to a world that does not truly threaten them, such a conceptualization is probably not appropriate. Rather than irrationality, elderly fear of crime may represent the exercise of caution by a group in society that frequently lacks the control necessary to manage the risk of criminal harm or to marshal the resources necessary to offset its consequences. (p.226)

Some local crime surveys in the UK make it very clear why older people in particular neighbourhoods fear crime:

Like other survey researchers we found a lower crime rate against older than younger people. However, we found that when assaults did occur against people over 45, the attack was more likely to involve severe violence ... they were more likely to be injured ... and the attack was more likely to have a greater effect on their lives. None of this supports the paradox of irrationality, often argued about older people and crime. (Young 1988, pp.170–1)

The decision, in this particular study, to define people aged over 45 as 'older' may have confused the discussion, however, as most commentators agree that even if elderly people spent more time outside at night, they would still be less likely to become victims of violent crime than younger people (see Clarke *et al.* 1985; Midwinter 1990).

Older people are concerned about crime not only on their own behalf but also experience 'social anxiety' about the dangers faced by the elderly in general (Jones 1987). Unlike the population at large, they express particular concern about two specific types of crime – burglary and vandalism. The fear of vandalism covers a wide range of anti-social behaviour, not all of which is illegal, and even unsuccessful attempts at burglary are extremely frightening for frail or housebound older people. The character of crime against older people is somewhat distinct from the pattern of crime against the person more generally. It often involves the exploitation of socially isolated victims in their own homes (Blunt 1993; Fattah and Sacco 1989) and old people are also particularly vulnerable to theft occurring as a result of fraudulent entry to their homes (Jones 1987). The case study below illustrates the impact of this type of crime.

Services for victims need to take into account the different needs of older people: 'the elderly warrant extra attention when they are the victims of crime, but attention which focuses on the reality of the crime, not attention which inflates its seriousness' (Mawby 1988, pp.108–9).

While older people would certainly benefit from more accurate information about the risk of victimisation than they commonly receive through the mass media, their fear is related to the seriousness of the consequences if they were to be victimised, as well as to the degree of risk they face (see Mawby and Gill 1987). When victimisation occurs, it often happens in the person's own home, which is perceived as a serious violation of privacy and feelings of safety and tends to highlight people's feelings of dependency and vulnerability (Jones 1987). Those older people who have been victimised once tend to fear repeated offences rather more than younger victims do. Older victims are less likely than crime victims in general to know 'their' offender or to be victimised outside the home (Fattah and Sacco 1989; Mawby 1988) and such information can be used in the prevention of further victimisation.

Case study

> Albert Jones is an 80-year-old widower living alone in a ground floor flat in a quiet residential area. He is referred to the local Victim Support scheme after he is tricked by a bogus caller into inviting him indoors, supposedly in order to check the gas supply for safety. While he is showing the young man the water heater in the bathroom, an accomplice climbs into the lounge from the rear of the house through an open window and takes money, medals and rings from the bureau.
>
> When the Victim Support volunteer calls a few days later she finds Mr Jones takes a long time to answer the door because he walks with the aid of sticks. Although it is a warm evening, he has all the windows closed and locked and asks for advice about intruder alarms, although he says he cannot really afford to have one installed. His pension money was collected the day before the burglary and was among the items stolen. He does not want an emergency loan but asks for help filling in a form applying for a grant from the Income Support office. He is making this application only out of desperation, regarding it as charity, and feels very bad about having to do so.
>
> He has no family in the immediate area but shows the volunteer photographs of his daughters and their children before going on to talk at some length about his fears of further victimisation and his feelings of anger and shame about being 'conned'. He says he has survived fighting

in World War Two and many years working in a dangerous job but now feels trapped in his own home.

They fill in the form together and the volunteer agrees to return the following week, although she feels this is more because of Albert's loneliness and vulnerability than any obvious need for practical support.

This case example illustrates a common form of crime against housebound older people: the offenders create a diversion to keep the victim out of the way while burgling his flat, using deception. As so often, the injured party feels foolish for having been taken in and resents having to apply to official-dom for help. Because he was not physically hurt, he is not eligible for financial compensation unless the offenders are caught, prosecuted and ordered to repay him – which is unlikely at best. He responds to victimisation by increasing the security of his property, which has the effect of making him feel like a captive. His self-sufficiency is threatened by having to depend on others to help him restore the equilibrium which existed before the crime. His vulnerability as an older person with restricted mobility has been exploited and he is likely to feel at risk and to keep up his vigilance for some time. The effect on his lifestyle may, indeed, be permanent.

Younger victims

Young people tend to be stereotyped as offenders but little attention is often paid to their needs as victims and their vulnerability to particular types of vic-timisation: 'Young people have long been positioned outside the boundaries of the "ideal victim". Official and popular discourse about crime tends to view young people as "trouble", rather than as regular users of public space vulnerable to its attendant risks' (Loader 1996, p.93).

Because young people 'hanging about' in groups are seen as problematic, and viewed as likely to be involved in anti-social incivility if not actual crime, there is little police or public sympathy for them when they are victimised. Their dependance upon public places for many of their leisure pursuits thus marginalises them and makes them much less inclined to report crime than older people, as Loader's (1996) interview data demonstrate – both the police and the young people he surveyed confirmed this (see also Anderson and Leitch 1996).

Crime surveys suggest, however, that young people experience high levels of criminal victimisation, both while out in public and from personal crime more generally.[9] Thefts and violence occurring between or against teenagers are unlikely to be reported or recorded as offences but where young people are asked about victimisation rates, they report relatively high levels of violent, sexual and personal theft offences (Levi 1994; Loader 1996; Mawby and Walklate 1994). Children clearly also suffer the consequences of property offences, such as house burglary, but their parents tend not to consider this separately from their own experience of victimisation and the police and victim agency volunteers are rarely trained in recognising or even looking out for traumatised children, except in the context of 'domestic' violence. This is surprising, given the prevalence of such assaults and of sexual harassment of young women (Anderson and Leitch 1996). In England and Wales Victim Support only began to accept referrals of child victims in 1990, and then only with parental consent. This followed a demonstration project by the Bedfordshire Victim Support scheme, where volunteers were specially trained in advising parents about child victims' likely reactions (Morgan and Zedner 1992).

There is evidence that children may suffer considerable trauma as a result of house burglaries: the security of the home is of considerable importance to many young people and its violation by a stranger creates a new and disturbing sense of vulnerability (Zedner 1994). This, along with other forms of indirect victimisation, such as children witnessing or otherwise affected by 'domestic' or other violence between adults, has only recently begun to be recognised (Morgan and Zedner 1992a). A survey of Victim Support schemes in two counties in the late 1980s found that a high proportion of burglaries involved families with children and that 'One in six burglaries took place whilst children were actually asleep in the house and in a small number of cases it was the child who ... discovered that the offence had taken place' (Morgan and Zedner 1992a, p.39).

The requirement that children obtain parental permission before contacting Victim Support appears to assume that parents are unlikely to be the perpetrators of offences against children, thus ignoring the whole issue of physical and sexual abuse. Perhaps understandably, VS argues that such cases are properly the responsibility of social services departments, which have

9   Loader (1996), citing two Scottish studies – Anderson et al. (1994) and Newburn (1997) discussing the British Crime Survey – and Kinsey and Anderson (1992)

statutory powers in this area. The complexity of the work is, perhaps, too great for a voluntary agency – yet Childline has been heavily involved with telephone counselling of child victims for some years. The existence of such a service is important because a major reason for the under-reporting of sexual offences against young people is 'manipulated fear and guilt' (Levi 1994, p.317). Any mechanism for the filtering of young victims, whether by the police, parents or victim agencies, is likely to make reporting more difficult for them unless it is specifically designed to be sensitive to the issue of child abuse. Child victims of crime have to overcome twin barriers: they have to 'earn' victim status by convincing parents or carers of their need for a response from the child care and criminal justice systems, and they have to convince the system that the offence against them is serious enough to merit intervention (Morgan and Zedner 1992a).

The resource implications of indirect victimisation of children are considerable: there are likely to be many more indirect than direct victims and it is unlikely that Victim Support and the other agencies concerned could cope with the work involved if all were to be referred to them. Training would also need to be given to existing and new staff and volunteers before such referrals could be taken on (see Morgan and Zedner 1992a).

Child sexual abuse is likely to lead to long-term trauma for victims (Newburn 1993). Like rape and other sexual offences against adults, it may remain undisclosed for many years: victims sometimes cope by losing their memory of the incidents involved or by keeping it to themselves. This means that services have to be sensitive to the possibility that other forms of victimisation may trigger memories of earlier abuse and, indeed, that work with victims may unleash powerful, buried feelings among volunteers and victim support workers. (Rape Crisis centres recognise this by making it clear during volunteer training that counselling survivors is likely to trigger memories of abusive relationships – and that, if necessary, counsellors are at liberty to revert to 'client' status while they receive help in dealing with this.)

Where abuse is disclosed when the victim is still a child, there is a sophisticated system of responses by official agencies and the issue of whether the offender should be criminalised is secondary to the best interests of the child or children concerned. This is a specialist area of social work not covered in any detail in this book but addressed in a number of other recent publications (see, for example, Morgan and Zedner 1992a; Owen and Pritchard 1993; Parton 1996).

Child victims have received relatively little attention, except in the case of victims of child abuse: 'The plight of child victims, indeed, their very existence, is only now being fully recognised. While this recognition led to the introduction of a number of innovations during the 1980s, much has still to be done in developing an adequate response to child victims' (Morgan and Zedner 1992, p.305).

Class and victimisation

Even officially recorded crime has a disproportionate impact upon poorer people – and if one were to try to quantify corporate and white-collar crime and add it to the figures, it would doubtless underline this message. A number of reasons for the unequal victimisation of the poor have been suggested. First, some of the groups particularly susceptible to victimisation themselves contain a high proportion of poorer people – women, disabled people and black people tend to be less well off than able-bodied white men. Membership of more than one of these 'vulnerable' groups multiplies one's chances of being victimised. Second, much crime is opportunist, so property and personal violence offenders will often victimise people in their own neighbourhoods, who tend – like them – to belong to the lower socio-economic groups.

Connected to this reason is another: the poor are easier targets for some types of crime because they cannot afford to protect themselves from it (for example, domestic burglary[10]) or because they live in crime-prone areas (which increases the likelihood of suffering such offences as street robberies and theft of and from vehicles).

As Young (1988) and other 'realist' criminologists have pointed out, aggregated crime figures create a rather misleading impression of the prevalence of victimisation at a local level. Only when surveys are carried out in small areas does a true picture emerge, and in poorer districts it is one of multiple victimisation and of a high proportion of offences which have a serious impact upon their victims. For this reason it is important to consider

---

10   Burglars tend to target two extremes of wealth, preying upon the poorest and the richest members of society. While unemployed people have the highest risk of domestic burglary, much of which is committed by opportunist offenders, high-income groups are particularly at risk from 'professional' burglars (Mawby and Walklate 1994).

the findings of local surveys alongside the national studies which lump all parts of the country together.

Local surveys have often been commissioned by councils and other local bodies responding to concern about crime, and they have generally been carried out in poorer parts of the country; Islington (which was a poor district of London in the 1980s when these surveys were carried out), Merseyside and Sheffield spring to mind. The surveys in these areas show that poorer people are indeed at high risk of criminal victimisation and that their lifestyles may be significantly affected by the fear and the reality of crime. People in poor inner-city areas not only fear crime, they experience it more frequently than the inhabitants of more prosperous areas and their lives are changed accordingly. This is not to suggest that there is a direct causal link between poverty or place of residence and crime or victimisation. People who live in poor areas may never be criminally victimised, but they are highly likely to know people who have been and this too will affect how safe they feel at home and in public. Many unemployed people never commit offences, but this does not mean that there is no relationship between the rates of unemployment and offending.

It is important to remember that criminal statistics are based upon cases processed by the courts and that some types of offending come to official attention in only a minority of cases. Particularly where violence within relationships is concerned, the incidents reaching official attention represent the tip of an iceberg. Cases actually taken to court are based upon specimen charges and often represent one serious incident in a history of years of abuse. As a number of researchers have pointed out, violence is so much a part of everyday experience for some victims that discussion of repeat victimisation rates is not only irrelevant but offensive in that context. The same will apply to many victims of racial and sexual harassment. The criminal justice system is designed to respond to discrete incidents, which in themselves may not seem serious, and sight can be lost of the bigger picture. The danger is that the desperation of people living under a constant shadow of violence and terror can be overlooked, which is why single-issue victims' organisations are so important.

A final, possibly rather obvious point needs to be made. This is that the impact of crime is higher for people who are already marginalised, so that relatively minor property offences have a disproportionate effect upon poorer people who cannot afford to sustain the losses involved. As Young (1994) puts it, 'The most vulnerable in our society are not only at the greatest risk of crime, but also suffer a greater impact of crime because of their lack of money and resources [and] the people who suffer most because of crime tend to suffer most from other social problems...' (p.113).

Disadvantaged victims are least able to shrug off the consequences of crime, yet they may not feel that it is worth reporting because they do not expect this to make their situation any better.

What about the criminals?

To conclude this discussion of the evidence in relation to differences in victimisation rates, it is worth briefly considering what is known about the characteristics of offenders. While generalisations can mislead, some general statements may assist understanding in this area.

First, there is a clear link between masculinity and offending: 'In general terms – and this holds true both across countries and across time – women commit fewer crimes of all types and proportionately fewer serious and violent crimes than men' (Newburn and Stanko 1994, p.1). This simple fact has been rather neglected by criminologists until quite recently, perhaps because it raises uncomfortable issues of power and gender. Those involved in helping victims cannot ignore the consequences of male anti-social behaviour and abuse of power if they are to offer genuinely empathic, authentic-feeling help to victims (a theme developed in Chapter Four).

Second, it is often the case that offenders are themselves criminally victimised. This is another simple fact which has been 'discovered' only recently. Victims and offenders are not two discrete groups, they overlap considerably (Peelo et al. 1992; Widom 1991). Thus Rape Crisis, Women's Aid and Victim Support find themselves counselling victims in prison and receiving referrals from probation officers to whom clients disclose abuse and victimisation. More than two-thirds of serious young offenders interviewed by Boswell disclosed childhood abuse (NAPO 1997). Prisoners' homes are often burgled while they are away and their partners may suffer various forms of victimisation too. It may be politically awkward to acknowledge that many victims of crime are not as pure as the driven snow themselves – and the issue is frequently avoided. But victims who themselves offend are, surely, entitled to help on the same basis as others who may superficially seem more deserving. Breaking down the artificial division between offenders and victims would also help to ensure that services to victims were appropriately targeted. For example, the UK criminal injuries compensation scheme, which is 'among the most restrictive in Europe', also tends to 'reflect the assumption that only the ideal innocent victim should benefit' (Joutsen 1987, p.284).

For many years the system of compensation for criminal injuries in the UK has perpetuated the differentiation of victims from offenders by refusing to compensate victims if they have a criminal record or by paying them reduced awards. The Criminal Injuries Compensation Board did decide in 1996, however, that people who were sexually abused as children and subsequently became offenders as adults should receive compensation for the abuse, albeit at a reduced level (Pallister 1996). It was argued in that case that their offending behaviour was influenced by their childhood abuse. Some of the reasons for the traditional strict differentiation between victims and offenders are discussed in Chapters One and Six.

A third, more widely known, fact is that those mainly responsible for recorded crime are poor, often unemployed and poorly educated. While poverty does not directly cause crime, there are indirect links between unemployment, drug misuse, truancy, low self-esteem, poor housing and crime (Drakeford and Vanstone 1996; Stewart *et al.* 1994). Victims may not welcome hearing sob stories about offenders but some do wish to understand what leads people to do cruel or selfish things and a few go further and try to help 'their' offenders.

A final characteristic worth considering is that a high proportion of offenders consists of people known to their victims. The figures are particularly striking in relation to more serious offences such as murder and rape. Most violence occurs in the context of personal relationships, rather than between complete strangers. This has been discussed above in the context of low reporting rates for 'domestic' violence and crime against older people. It has implications for prosecution policies and for service delivery to victims.

If criminal prosecution is intended partly as a symbol of social disapproval of offending, a political decision can be made to prosecute all reported cases of a particular type of socially unacceptable behaviour. An example is the decision to respond decisively to all complaints of spouse abuse, as in the zero tolerance campaign conducted in Winnipeg, Canada (Ursel 1994). A separate family violence court was established there in 1990 and it has led to child abuse and domestic violence being taken more seriously – in particular, offenders are now more likely to be imprisoned for very short periods and more likely to receive long probation orders with conditions of attendance at alcohol misuse or batterers' groups. The court also provides victim and witness support services, ensuring sympathetic treatment of complainants (Schulman 1997).

British commentators have been sceptical about whether such a strategy would succeed here (Cretney and Davis 1995) but Edinburgh District Council has successfully emulated Ontario's public awareness campaign against domestic violence and sexual assault (see Kitzinger and Hunt 1993). Although this consisted only of an advertising campaign, developed in consultation with victims' organisations, its long-term aims were to highlight the need for adequate support services and legal protection for women and children, debunk myths about male violence to women and children, and 'promote a criminalisation strategy' (Kitzinger and Hunt 1993, p.5). The project was repeated in London by Islington's local authority, followed in 1994 by a national advertising campaign funded by the Home Office, which was criticised for failing to tackle the underlying policy issues or to fund women's refuges adequately (Smith 1993; Travis 1994).

In terms of work with identified victims, the fact that a high proportion of victims of violence have suffered at the hands of known assailants affects the ways in which services are delivered. Volunteer visitors need protection from potential danger when visiting clients' homes or (preferably) appropriate cases need to be identified in advance so that meetings with victims can be arranged at neutral venues. This is routinely done by the main victim support agencies and, as well as providing a safe meeting place, it gives greater privacy than home visits would allow. The existence of specialist agencies to assist in cases of spouse abuse and sexual assault allows referral between the various voluntary organisations but inter-agency relationships are, on occasions, competitive rather than co-operative (see Chapter One).

The significance of this brief survey of what is known about offenders is that it again draws attention to the dynamics of victimisation, which are considerably more complex than is often assumed. In Chapter Three the needs of victims are considered, along with the likely effects of different types of crime, and this complexity again becomes apparent.

The Needs of Victims of Crime

The needs of victims vary according to the type of crime involved and this chapter examines some common reactions to victimisation and the ways in which support and help can appropriately be offered in a range of circumstances. Case studies will be discussed at some length to illustrate some of the issues involved in responding to the victims of the more common types of offences.

Once again, it must be emphasised that people's reactions to being victimised are individual and unpredictable. While there are some discernible patterns, it can never be assumed that a particular offence will have predictable consequences for an individual victim. Generalisations are used in this chapter for explanatory purposes but they are not intended to imply homogeneous victim responses – in practice, people respond to victimisation in diverse and sometimes surprising ways. All the same, it can be useful for those involved in supporting victims to have an idea of 'typical' responses and victims themselves may be reassured to know that their reaction is a common or familiar one.

Common reactions to victimisation

As the case studies in Chapter Two showed, victims of crime may feel fear, shame, resentment, anger against the offender and the criminal justice system, humiliation and a variety of other emotions. They may wish to be proactive, protecting themselves from further offences, or the experience may disempower them and make them feel – at least temporarily – less able to cope. In some cases they withdraw into themselves and retreat from painful reminders of what they have experienced or simply refuse to believe that it has happened. Crime, particularly, but not only if it is serious, can call cherished assumptions into question: what seemed like a safe, orderly world is suddenly threatening and unpredictable. Victims may feel physically ill, they often find it difficult to sleep and to concentrate, they are jumpy and easily startled, they may lose interest in favourite activities and in people close to them, and their self-esteem and social lives may suffer. In severe cases they want to move out of the house or completely away from the area where they were victimised, and long-term reactions such as depression and post-traumatic stress reactions may occur.

These responses are normal, however illogical they sometimes seem. Just as guilt is a usual part of the process of bereavement, even despite the lack of any rational basis for feeling guilty about one's relationship with the person who has died, so victimisation has its typical emotional responses, which are functional in helping victims to regain their equilibrium. Naturally, these vary between individuals and in intensity.

While a sensitive response to a victim expressing such feelings would obviously involve accepting how he or she feels, it can also, in some circumstances, be helpful gently to question some responses as part of the recovery process. For example, if someone who has been sexually assaulted feels guilty about their handling of the incident, they may need to be reassured that they behaved appropriately and that it is invariably the perpetrator, not the victim, who is at fault in such situations. Many victims of sexual abuse are prevented from reporting the assaults by the perpetrator's manipulation of their feelings of guilt and shame, and it can help, when they do disclose their abuse, to provide an opportunity to consider the dynamics of such situations and who is really at fault. Referral to self-help groups, or other settings where victims have an opportunity to compare notes, often helps to reduce feelings of isolation and of being set apart from people whose sense of security remains unviolated.

Victims' reactions to common offence types

Victim Support workers and volunteers spend most of their time responding to victims of burglary. Because it is so common, and because individual reactions to being burgled differ considerably, burglary will be used as a case study of victims' reaction to common types of offence. Some people quickly get back into their stride after a burglary but the case study examines a fairly common experience of recovery taking rather longer.

Case study

Mildred is a widow aged 80 and lives alone. Her house has been burgled twice in just over a year. On each occasion entry was gained through the back gate, which overlooks a park. After the first break-in, Mildred's son fitted window locks, but the second burglary was committed on a hot day when the windows were left open while Mildred went to the corner shop.

When she got home, Mildred found that the whole house had been quickly and carelessly searched. Her wedding ring, some other jewellery, various ornaments, all the money she had left in the house and the video player were missing. Although covered by insurance, some of the stolen items had strong personal associations and were irreplaceable. For Mildred, the invasion of her home and the fear that the offenders might return when she was there were more important than the loss sustained. She also felt very foolish about leaving windows open. The police referred her to the local Victim Support scheme and, a few days later, a volunteer named Eddie phoned. She told him that she had coped with a burglary before and said that there was no need for him to visit.

However, she felt more and more uncomfortable about leaving the house empty. When at home, she was so preoccupied with securing doors and windows that she felt rather trapped, particularly when alone and in warm weather. She found herself thinking more about her late husband, reminded of him by the theft of the wedding ring, although it was many years since his death. She increasingly avoided going out. For some weeks she had difficulty sleeping and had nightmares. The overall effect of the burglary included a measure of depression and a reduction in Mildred's quality of life, despite her determination to cope without outside intervention.

Maguire and Bennett (1982) found that 65 per cent of the burglary victims they interviewed were still affected by the offence four to ten weeks after it occurred. More of them complained of feelings of intrusion and other emotional effects than those who said that the financial loss was the worst aspect of the offence. Although the experience of Victim Support schemes is that many domestic burglary victims do not take up the offer of a visit from a volunteer, it is not known whether those who do receive such a visit fare any better than victims who refuse. In Mildred's case a relatively minor offence is aggravated by the facts that she lives alone and that she has been burgled before. Her age may (but will not necessarily) increase her feelings of vulnerability. Such factors tend to increase the impact of crime (Maguire 1980; see also Mayhew, Elliott and Dowds 1989 and Chapter Two). In some cases people reluctantly decide to move house, sometimes leaving an area in which they have lived for many years, because of repeated burglaries. It is also quite common for previous traumatic events to resurface in victims' minds when reacting to an offence, as in the case of Mildred's rekindled grief for her late husband.

Some people undoubtedly do respond in a robust way and put burglaries quickly behind them, but others are troubled for a long period and a few never fully recover from the trauma. Extreme reactions are particularly likely where the victim is already under stress from different sources, and this applies to many minor offences as well as burglary. Property offences are relatively serious for anyone of limited income, for whom small losses may have considerable consequences. The financial value of items stolen is often less important than their personal value to the victim, as with Mildred's jewellery and ornaments.

Families' reactions to the murder of a loved one

People affected by very serious crimes, not surprisingly, experience particularly strong reactions. While many people can shrug off something like a burglary or the theft of a car and continue with their lives more or less unaffected, the loss of a relative at the hands of a violent offender has a profound and permanent impact. Although the victimisation in these cases is secondary – the direct victim is dead – it has extreme consequences.

Unfortunately, the criminal justice system often makes things worse and survivors of murder victims may feel extremely angry with the system and all its representatives because of that experience. The way in which such secondary victims are treated needs careful thought and planning by everyone involved at every stage, but, at present, this does not always take place.

Completely inadvertent behaviour can be experienced as insensitive – for example, when professionals contact the family around the time of the anniversary of the victim's death without making reference to the significance of the date (Home Office 1996a). In some ways, though, the criminal justice system is structured in such a way as actively to cause murder victims' survivors additional suffering: criminal trials, for example, often involve scrutiny of victims' lifestyles and damaging or embarrassing impressions may be given without surviving relatives or friends having any right of reply. In other ways the system increases the pain through lack of thought or foresight, as when family members are summoned to give evidence and then not required, or when cases are repeatedly adjourned without explanation or notice.

Family members may be interviewed many times by the police in the aftermath of a murder, sometimes even regarded as suspects, and this is extremely hurtful at a desperately difficult time. Attending a criminal trial, even with the assistance of members of a Witness Support scheme, can be very traumatic for people who knew the victim and may be unfamiliar with the workings of the system. They may welcome comfort and advice offered by others who have been through the same experience: it can be helpful to make survivors aware of the existence of Victim Support and self-help organisations such as SAMM (Support After Murder and Manslaughter) (see Yorath 1995), Parents of Murdered Children and Cruse, as well as Victim Support's Witness Service.

When a murderer (among other types of serious offenders) is being considered for release, the probation service is required, under the terms of the Victim's Charter, to consult the victim's family. This provision was recommended by Victim Support as a result of its evaluation of a pilot project in which families of murder victims were offered support (Brown, Christie and Morris 1990). Although few victims' relatives wanted the burden of taking part in decision making about offenders' futures, most wanted to be kept informed and to be consulted about where the offender would live on release. It took some time for the new arrangements to be implemented and there were teething problems in some areas, which undoubtedly caused unnecessary distress to relatives who were unexpectedly contacted by probation staff years after a murder. Although area probation services still deal with such cases in a variety of different ways, staff training and awareness of victims' and survivors' feelings and needs have improved (Nettleton, Walklate and Williams 1997), and the service is welcomed by many victims and survivors because it responds to the need for information and a degree of involvement in the decision-making process (see Chapter Five for a more detailed description of probation responsibilities for victim contact and support).

Victims' survivors often say that, unlike direct victims of crime, they expect never to recover – it is all but impossible to put the deliberate, violent death of a loved one behind you and many survivors have no wish to do so. People working with survivors need to hear this message – it is impertinent to assume that one knows best and that time, somehow, should heal. It is not for those offering support to victims and survivors to tell them when it is time to 'move on', particularly when their grief is likely to be aggravated by the knowledge that the perpetrator of the offence is still alive – a feeling brought back to the surface when enquiries are made about perpetrators' release or rehabilitation arrangements (Parkes 1993). Murder victims' survivors are likely to be suffering not only from grief but, in some cases, also from post-traumatic stress syndrome or something akin to it (Masters, Friedman and Getzel 1988). The process of coming to terms with the profound changes caused by extreme victimisation of this kind is necessarily a longer one, and a more complex one, than might be expected in the case of victims of lesser harm.

Case study

Albert and Mary lost their daughter, Susan, in 1984. Susan's ex-partner, hearing that she had started going out with another man, had broken into her house at night and, in the course of a violent struggle, killed her. Albert and Mary found the loss extremely difficult to cope with, but their grief was aggravated by the insensitive and bureaucratic treatment they received from various agencies of the criminal justice system.

They were themselves questioned repeatedly, and at some length, by the police in the days after Susan's body was found and, for a time, it felt as though they were suspected of the murder. When an arrest was made, they only found out from the local evening newspaper. They were not told when the man accused of the crime was to appear for trial but found out by calling the Crown Court office every week until they were told that the trial was listed. They had to clear out their daughter's house after her death and subsequently avoided the area where she had lived because going there brought painful memories to the surface. For a long time, Mary contacted both her sons several times a day to check that nothing dreadful had happened to either of them.

Attending court, the couple heard distressing details of the injuries inflicted on their daughter and the pain she had suffered before her death, as well as previously unknown 'facts' about her social and sexual activities. The barrister defending the accused man attempted to imply that Susan had invited her assailant into her house and that she had provoked the murder. Although the murderer changed his plea to guilty, thus shortening the trial, Albert and Mary both had nightmares about their daughter's final hours for many months after the trial. They talked about the case all the time and some friends began to tire of this and avoid them.

More than ten years later, when they had begun to cope again, they received a letter from the local probation service saying that the offender had expressed interest in resettling in the area after his release, and offering to take their views into account. Albert did not wish to respond, but Mary thought they should and, eventually, they agreed to receive a visit from the probation officer. When she came, they were surprised and upset to discover that she knew their daughter's killer quite well and had been visiting him in prison for some years. They strongly expressed the view that he should never be released, but the probation officer explained that this was not the issue about which they were being consulted. Their opinion was sought solely on the question of where he should live and what conditions should be imposed if he were to be released. She gave them leaflets setting out the provisions of the Victim's Charter and said that it was her job to hear their views and pass them on to the prison authorities, if they agreed to this.

Mary and Albert said that the offender had better not come anywhere near the area: their sons would be on the look out for him. But they felt that the system was more interested in the interests and rights of the murderer than in their feelings and those of their sons. The probation officer said that she could understand that they might feel that way and suggested that they make contact with Victim Support: she explained that it was an independent organisation concerned with the needs and rights of victims of crime. She also offered to meet the two sons and wrote giving them an appointment, although they reacted by sending a strongly-worded reply saying they wanted nothing to do with her or anyone else who cosseted murderers.

Mary rang the local Victim Support scheme, initially more interested in obtaining allies in preventing her daughter's killer from being released than in receiving emotional support. The scheme's co-ordinator arranged for a volunteer to visit. A few days later, the volunteer, Steve, called to see Mary and Albert. After a couple of lengthy discussions over the next week, he offered to remain involved but also suggested that they consider contacting the local group of SAMM, a self-help and campaigning group which works with survivors of murder victims. It was agreed that he would bring Janine from SAMM with him next time he visited.

After several visits from Janine at her home, Mary gradually became involved in SAMM's activities herself. She felt that by helping others who had suffered similar losses, she was giving Susan's life and death continuing meaning. Increasingly, she also came to enjoy her social contacts with other members outside formal meetings. From Janine she also obtained help in making representations through her Member of Parliament to the Home Office, succeeding in arguing for a condition in the offender's release licence that he be required to live in a different part of the country.

This was not the end of the story by any means. Albert became increasingly depressed and withdrawn and was diagnosed as suffering from high blood pressure which was thought to be stress-related. While Mary found her involvement in SAMM fulfilling, Albert was impatient and angry when she tried to discuss it with him and refused to become involved himself. They both continued to have painful and unwelcome thoughts about their daughter's death and to feel that nothing could be finally settled while the murderer remained alive. Albert found himself preoccupied with revenge, while Mary felt that her work with SAMM was of vital importance in providing others with the kind of practical advice and emotional support that had not been available to her and Albert in the immediate aftermath of the murder.

The differing reactions displayed by Mary and Albert illustrate the individual nature of responses to traumatic events. This will depend upon personal attributes as well as on the relationship between the individual and the victim, and different attitudes and reactions can cause (or aggravate) difficulties in personal relationships.

As noted earlier, many survivors of murder victims undergo a kind of post-traumatic stress and there is some evidence of this in the case study. Intrusive thoughts, emotional turbulence, intense pain over a prolonged period of time, avoidance of situations which reminded them of the murder, withdrawal from contact with friends who do not share a similar experience and psychosomatic medical symptoms are all signs of post-traumatic stress exhibited by Albert and Mary. Their case also illustrates the unpredictability of recovery after such a trauma: there is no orderly, predictable progress towards normality. Rather, events and situations years later can trigger another episode of grief – including reminders of the continued survival of the murderer (for more detailed discussion of the 'psychodynamics of guilt and rage', see Masters, Friedman and Getzel 1988).

The need for repetitive discussion of the traumatic event, which becomes tedious to friends, is part of the recovery process. When Mary found people, in SAMM, who would listen with genuine empathy and without being judgemental about her need to go over the same ground repeatedly, she discovered a healthy way of expressing her grief. This kind of help can also be provided by other voluntary organisations, such as Victim Support or Cruse, and by mental health professionals (see Parkes 1993).

Surviving a younger relative is a particularly poignant reminder of the uncertainty of human life and raises issues concerning the survivors' mortality. Trauma and loss remind us that everything we take for granted is unreliable (and one of the reasons that friends may avoid the bereaved is from fear of being reminded that they, too, are vulnerable and mortal). The carefully constructed mechanisms which give us an illusion of control over our lives are shattered by bereavement and this can easily lead to depression and feelings of being alone, as in Albert's case. Or it may provoke a reappraisal of the survivor's value system and a reaching out towards constructive ways of responding, as with Mary's voluntary work for SAMM, which followed a period as a 'client' during which she received reassurance that someone cared about her loss and that it had meaning. Mary's response was more functional than Albert's in that she began to rebuild the 'assumptive world' which was threatened by the murder of her daughter (Erikson 1976). Albert's anger towards Mary for her increasing involvement in SAMM at least served the purpose of allowing him to turn his feelings outwards, rather than internalising his anger and making himself physically ill.

Practices have changed over the last decade and the insensitive response from the police experienced by Albert and Mary should now be less common (Mawby and Walklate 1994; Nettleton, Walklate and Williams 1997), although an important minority of victims of particular types of offending continue to complain of police insensitivity (Lees 1997; Temkin 1996). Police procedure in murder cases is always likely to reflect the fact that many such offences are committed by people close to the victim and relatives are bound to be offended to discover that they are under suspicion. The treatment of victims of sexual offences, who also remain dissatisfied with police procedures in many instances, is discussed further in the next section and in Chapters Four and Five, with case studies.

Those working with offenders can be perceived as insensitive and uncaring simply because they misjudge the victim's readiness to engage in discussion about the perpetrator. Some victims and survivors are remarkably forgiving – they may even express concern about the offender's welfare.

Others need to express feelings of rage and guilt to someone in authority and it is unhelpful if police or probation staff react defensively or by giving them prescriptive advice about how they should behave. Such authority figures may be temperamentally inclined to try and control situations where people complain about the system or threaten to do illegal things in revenge for the wrong done to them but they should resist the temptation to fall back upon their authority as a defence against victims' emotions.

Probation officers have been encouraged, in recent years, to 'confront offending behaviour'. This needs to be done carefully and sensitively if it is to have any influence upon offenders' future attitudes and behaviour. It will rarely be appropriate for anyone working with victims to engage in a similar kind of confrontation (Aubrey and Hossack 1994). The officer in the case study was right to encourage the couple to talk to a Victim Support volunteer, although Mary subsequently found a more congenial source of long-term support. Involving an independent organisation was more constructive than attempting to defend the policies the probation service has to implement.

It appears that a form of confrontation can, however, be helpful to victims if the timing is judged correctly. The expression of anger and self-blame is necessary first, and may be needed again, but there can come a time when it does become appropriate to confront the victim or survivor with the consequences for them of isolating themselves from people around them (Masters, Friedman and Getzel 1988). It takes sensitivity and experience to judge such situations, although it is easier to get away with apparent insensitivity if one has been working with someone for a relatively long time and trust has built up. Meier and Davis (1993) (see also Williams 1996) suggest that: 'A good rule of thumb is that you can confront as much as you've supported ... confrontation is unwise during the early stages of counseling. However, once you have established a bond, confrontation may increase client self-awareness and motivation to change' (p.12).

People are more likely to forgive apparent insensitivity if there is already a strong relationship between them and the worker concerned. The choice of a supportive worker or volunteer must be left to victims and survivors themselves, and they need information about all the options open to them. Thankfully, murder is comparatively rare. We now turn to a much more common type of offence: rape.

Helping rape survivors

In this chapter the work of Victim Support schemes with survivors of rape is considered. In Chapters Four and Five further case studies will examine the work of other agencies, such as Rape Crisis centres. As with other types of victimisation, responses to rape vary considerably between individuals.

One of the most difficult decisions for a woman who has been raped, and one about which she is likely to seek advice (although not always in the immediate aftermath of the event), is whether or not to report the offence to the police. While no general guidance is likely to be helpful in all cases, it is important that people advising survivors are aware of the way in which the criminal justice system operates and of the obstacles to convicting rapists (Jenkins 1997; Lees 1997). Once an allegation has been made to the police, the matter is taken out of the hands of the person reporting it, and this is more problematic in rape cases than where other types of offence are concerned. The sense of helplessness when police and lawyers take over can be quite disempowering, especially when an independent-minded complainant wishes to be involved in decisions about the case and her views are not taken into account. The advice of people experienced in dealing with rape cases should be drawn upon in all such cases, or else the survivor should be directly referred to an appropriate group, such as Rape Crisis.

There can be no doubt that the criminal justice system handles allegations of rape insensitively in many cases. There is evidence that administrative and procedural changes can alleviate this situation only to a limited extent as attitudes towards rape have their origins in patriarchal assumptions about women's sexuality (Lees 1996, 1997; T. 1988; Whalen 1996;) and change in this area is bound to be slow, resisted as it is by a male establishment and the individual vested interests of men. Matters are further complicated by the entrenched, macho subculture of the police in most countries.

An example is the treatment of people who do decide to report rape by the police and doctors. The legal establishment was made aware of concern about the issue in the 1970s (see, for example, Heilbron Committee 1975), but the crass and obnoxious attitudes of many investigating detectives and police surgeons were exposed to a wider public in the early 1980s by Roger Graef's television documentary about the Thames Valley Police. The public reaction to this film meant that changes had to be made and the police responded by training specialist staff, involving more women doctors and police officers in investigating rapes and setting up investigation suites where statements could be taken in relatively comfortable and reassuring surroundings.

While these improvements were important, there is evidence that underlying attitudes may not have changed as much as the administrative changes might lead one to expect. Many women reporting rape are still being examined by male doctors, and given no choice in the matter. Medical examinations by male and female doctors are perceived as insensitive in a substantial proportion of cases, with questions which have already been asked by the police repeated for reasons which are not obvious to complainants. Thus some rape survivors continue to state that they found the process of being examined 'more degrading and demoralising than the rape itself' (Temkin 1996, p.18) or that the doctor made them feel more like an object than a person (Lees 1997).

As for police investigations, rape complainants continue to be aggrieved that they are not kept informed of progress or of the reasons for forensic procedures involving intimate examinations and samples. However, the practice in some police areas of assigning a female officer to act as the survivor's link with the system seems to be working well (Lees 1997; Nuttall and Morrison 1997). Decisions by prosecuting authorities to downgrade rape cases (often as a result of plea bargains, where offenders agree to admit lesser charges) cause considerable anger and distress for women who have made the difficult decision to report rape. The experience of giving evidence in contested cases remains likely to be a very difficult one and lawyers' aggressive questioning has not been substantially curbed.

Case study

Andrea is referred to her local Victim Support scheme by the police after reporting being raped by a work colleague. She is contacted by Eleanor, an experienced volunteer who has received specialist training and also attends the local scheme's Sexual Violence Support Group regularly. Eleanor offers to visit Andrea at her home and she agrees.

When Eleanor comes to see her, Andrea is very clear that she needs practical help in dealing with the consequences of the attack but no more. They discuss the danger that the perpetrator may have passed sexually-transmitted diseases on to Andrea, the procedure for claiming under the compensation scheme and how to find out about the progress of the case. Andrea wants to make most of the arrangements herself but

THE NEEDS OF VICTIMS OF CRIME

she asks Eleanor to go with her when she attends the Genito-Urinary Clinic to be tested.

Eleanor agrees to make the appointment for Andrea and goes with her a few days later. She calls on her at home the following week and Andrea thanks her for her efforts and says that the results were negative. Her mind is at rest and she is ready to deal with the other aspects of the case herself. Eleanor tells her how impressed she is with the way she has dealt with things, reminds her that she is still available if she can be of any further assistance (and of how to contact her) and they say their goodbyes.

This case study demonstrates the individuality of people's responses to victimisation. Andrea found one aspect of the aftermath of the rape particularly distressing and distasteful, and Eleanor was able to support her through it. That apart, Andrea wanted to handle things herself and Eleanor respected her decision. At this stage, Andrea is not asking explicitly for emotional support, but Eleanor has left the door open and, should Andrea feel the need to approach Victim Support again in future, she knows that it will be Eleanor who responds. A very brief, focused intervention has potentially set the scene for further support in future if it should be needed.

This case study (along with the next one) shows the flexibility of voluntary organisations such as Victim Support. Although they have established procedures and expertise, they do not try to fit victims and survivors into preordained categories or 'treatment plans'. Their approach is to build upon simple good neighbourliness, and train some volunteers specifically to work with survivors of serious crime. If an individual wants to seek only a specified type of support, and it is within the volunteer's power to provide this, the wishes of the individual are respected.

Some people suffer severe, long-term disruption as the result of being raped. Others recover remarkably quickly and want to get back to normal and show the perpetrator and others that they remain in control of their life. Services to survivors need to recognise this range of responses.

Case study

The next referral Eleanor received from her Victim Support co-ordinator turned out to be a very different experience from supporting Andrea when she visited the clinic. Samantha was 17. She had accepted a lift home from an acquaintance she met on leaving a club one night because he lived near her. He subjected her to a violent and humiliating sexual assault in the car and abandoned her in a lay-by. She reported the attack to the police as soon as she could find a phone and, after she was questioned overnight and examined at some length by a male doctor, the offender was prosecuted and remanded in custody. He denied the offence and there was to be a trial. Samantha was very frightened of going to court and seeing the offender face to face. Although the police were extremely supportive initially, they did not keep in regular contact with Samantha and she found it difficult to find out what was going on.

Eleanor provided long-term support, arranging for Samantha to visit the court before the trial, going with her each time the case was in court, contacting the police and the court regularly for information, helping her with a claim for compensation and seeing her regularly for emotional support. Court dates were fixed and then altered at the last minute on two occasions, after Samantha had prepared herself to give evidence, and Eleanor supported her through this. When the case finally came to court, the defence barrister made repeated references to Samantha's previous boyfriends and attempted to prove that she had led the offender to believe that she wanted to have sex with him. Her request to be allowed to give evidence from behind a screen was refused, but she was determined to cope with being cross-examined. Contact between Eleanor and Samantha continued after the trial (at which two offences were proved and the man received a four-year prison sentence) because Samantha became very depressed and withdrawn and had told none of her friends about her ordeal. She no longer wanted to go out dancing – indeed, at first, she was anxious about leaving the house at all – and had twice had anxiety attacks as a result of 'flashbacks' where she involuntarily recalled details of the attack when meeting male friends. She felt very ashamed about what her parents had heard during the trial and blamed herself for causing them embarrassment.

After a few months of regular contact, Eleanor began to see some signs of improvement and Samantha agreed to her suggestion that they no longer needed to meet so often. Eventually, they stopped making appointments and Samantha was left to initiate contact, which she did from time to time, particularly after being contacted by a probation officer about the offender's possible future release. She gradually resumed her social life and, two years after the offence, received a substantial cheque from the Criminal Injuries Compensation Authority.

Samantha's case was a relatively straightforward one from the police point of view in that there was a known offender (who had been arrested before in connection with a similar matter, although Samantha did not find this out until the trial was over) and forensic evidence was found to substantiate the complaint. This, of course, did not mean that her own reactions were any less complex or distressing. She was automatically referred to Victim Support and the response was swift and effective. Had she decided not to report the matter to the police, no such help would have been offered unless she requested it herself (and knew it was available). Increasing numbers of rape survivors are contacting support agencies directly rather than as a result of referral by the police (Victim Support 1996a) and there is a variety of organisations which can offer appropriate help, including the Samaritans and Rape Crisis centres.

Like a substantial proportion of survivors of rape, Samantha experienced depression and showed signs of post-traumatic stress (Mezey 1988; Newburn 1993). Eleanor's non-judgemental support, and her reassurance that Samantha's reactions were normal, helped her to recover. Eleanor recognised the signs that Samantha was entering a 'reorganizational stage' (Mezey 1988), putting the confusion and distress gradually behind her, and was able to help her to decide what needed to be done to get her life back on an even keel. For Samantha, the sentence the offender received (although it seemed lenient, it was at least formal recognition that the man was dangerous and that he should be punished for what he had done to her), and the payment of compensation, were important stages in her recovery.

But the recovery process is a long-term one and is unlikely to be smooth or predictable. Some survivors are distraught when offenders are acquitted, or receive lenient sentences, and when they receive what they regard as insultingly low levels of compensation for injuries sustained. Anyone who has experienced the level of stress involved in such an assault is likely to find that there are unexpected setbacks to their recovery process. Where there are pre-existing problems (such as previous victimisation, psychiatric illness or substance misuse), the 'reorganizational stage' may take longer to arrive, if it ever comes (Mezey 1988). It is clearly important to arrange services to survivors in such a way that they can drop in and out as they feel the need, and individual personal relationships are very important. Not all survivors are able to 'reorganise' their lives as Samantha did and the voluntary agencies provide lifetime support for a minority of those with whom they work.

In extreme cases referral to professional services may be considered, although some of those in the voluntary agencies feel that professionals are not always sufficiently responsive to users' needs. This issue is considered more fully in Chapter Five.

In this chapter brief case studies have been used to illustrate the types of help available from Victim Support volunteers. Some of the more specialist agencies feature in the case studies in Chapter Five. Meanwhile, Chapter Four returns to the theme of the politics of victimisation and takes victim policy in the United Kingdom as an example of attempts by the central state to co-opt pressure group interests for its own political ends.

The Politics of Victimisation

This chapter continues the examination of the increasing politicisation of discussions about victims of crime, begun in Chapter One, and goes on to consider the effect this has had upon victim services. The role of the voluntary sector in meeting victims' needs and arguing for their rights is considered. Some of the voluntary agencies depend upon central government for much of their funding and this inevitably constrains their outspokenness on policy issues. Nevertheless, they too have been part of the process of politicising victims' issues, and this process is discussed. The role and purpose of the Victim's Charter is analysed: was it intended to increase the rights of victims of crime or to make the criminal justice system seem fairer and more legitimate in victims' eyes without substantially changing it? Does the language of consumer rights fit appropriately with the kind of rights being demanded by organisations working with victims of crime?

The process of politicising victims' issues and some possible reasons for it

In Chapter One the historical and political context of increasing political interest in victims of crime in America and Europe was briefly considered. It was suggested that while politicians might be willing to use the rhetoric of giving greater priority to the rights and needs of victims, the practical consequences for victims of the changes made were not always readily apparent or predictable. Even when legal and administrative changes were made in the name of supporting victims of crime, they often did not seem to lead to real change. There is clearly a danger that merely symbolic changes may be made (Weed 1995) and a linked concern that policies aimed at improving victims' situation may worsen the position of offenders in ways that do not help victims in the longer term. Some changes made with the aim of improving victims' position may even make it worse. Later in this chapter these issues will be examined more fully with reference to the Victim's Charter. First, the reasons for the politicisation of victims' issues are considered in greater detail.

The identification of social problems is a complex process and it is not always clear why a particular issue seizes the imagination of politicians, the media or the public at a given time. In the case of issues relating to victims of crime there are genuine concerns which need addressing, but there is also an element of political manipulation or exploitation of these issues. Victims served a political purpose for New Right politicians wishing to shift the agenda away from the rehabilitation of offenders towards their punishment, to encourage a harsher sentencing climate and one in which criminal justice professionals could be brought under firmer central government control. It may also be that political speeches about the neglect of victims served to distract attention from the enormous and rapidly growing expenditure on prisons, both in Europe and North America.

The areas of concern about the criminal justice system have been discussed in earlier chapters: victims are frequently marginalised, sometimes completely ignored and, often, further victimised as a result of the responses to their victimisation, including both the responses of criminal justice systems around the world and those arising from popular attitudes. The damage done by offenders is, often, not even partially put right and the experience of providing evidence in criminal proceedings can feel as bad as, or even worse than, the original victimisation in some cases. What evidence is there that victims of crime have also become the victims of political cynicism?

Some of the arguments of Robert Elias were discussed in Chapter One and there is no need to go over the same ground again, except to reiterate that his analysis stands up to critical scrutiny. Politicians have mounted 'wars' on drugs and crime in the name of protecting victims and potential victims of crime and there is little evidence that this has had the effects which were the declared intention of such policies. Such wars have been expensive to fight, have done nothing to reduce victimisation rates and have criminalised huge numbers of people without doing anything to change their attitudes or behaviour. They have, however, helped politicians to appear tough on crime (Elias 1993; Jones 1996; Phipps 1988).

Laws aimed at protecting victims and enhancing their rights have been passed but, in many cases, not enforced (Lees 1997; Moxon 1993; Wemmers 1996). Resources have been diverted from the treatment of offenders, which might have had some long-term impact upon victimisation rates, to cover the cost of higher rates of incarceration. The funding of victim support agencies and compensation schemes has also been cut. Financial support has been channelled towards the assistance of 'ideal' victims at the expense of less popular and 'deserving' groups, despite the real unmet needs of those seen as less eligible (Walklate 1989).

Nevertheless, there has been a considerable increase in legislative and political activity on victims' issues since the 1970s (see Appendix). In some cases constructive change has undoubtedly resulted. But the number of unenforced laws and unresourced initiatives must lead one to question the sincerity of some of those taking these political initiatives.

It may be that one motive underlying the introduction of ultimately ineffective victim protection legislation is a desire to 'buy off' the emerging victims' movement. If so, this is a risky political strategy and one which is unlikely to succeed in the long term. Victims and victims' organisations are likely to become increasingly disgruntled and, perhaps, more politically active if they feel that their demands are being ignored. Similar consequences are likely if it appears that governments are pursuing a policy of minimal compliance with their obligations, passing laws simply to pacify the victims' movement or to conform to international conventions and treaties but with no real intention of providing sufficient resources to enforce them. This is all conjecture, however, and it would be difficult to prove with any degree of certainty that politicians have deliberately passed weak legislation.

What clearly has happened is that certain sections of the victims' movement have been favoured at the expense of others. Politicians, as well as the police and other local criminal justice agencies, find it easier to work with some types of victims' organisations than with others. In particular, anti-racist and feminist-influenced agencies in the UK are uncongenial to many in the police, probation and crown prosecution services, and to central government. The Home Office soon made clear its distrust of 'more militant feminist alternatives' to Victim Support as they emerged in the late 1970s (Mawby and Walklate 1994). One consequence has been that funding for Victim Support increased considerably while organisations such as Rape Crisis centres, racial harassment projects and Women's Aid refuges have been starved of public money. Formal relationships exist between local Victim

Support schemes and the police, probation and social services throughout the country but few similar agreements cover these agencies' links with the smaller victims' agencies. This cuts off access, not only to local funding opportunities but also to communication routes, for the referral of victims needing services (Hague *et al.* 1995; Nettleton, Walklate and Williams 1997; Williams 1996a).

Thus some sections of the victim support movement are being denied resources for political reasons and victims are prevented from gaining access to services which might be more suitable for their needs than those to which they are referred by official organisations, particularly by the police. Victims of sexual and domestic violence and of racial harassment and violence are less likely than other victims to report offences to the police and, therefore, less likely to be referred to Victim Support. If they were aware of the confidential services offered by women's organisations and agencies assisting victims of racial violence, they might well want to use them, but these groups are denied publicity and official legitimacy as well as funding. The channelling of resources towards those victims and organisations seen as more deserving results from an idealised image of an 'innocent victim' (Strobl 1997; Walklate 1989; see also Chapter One), which leads to the denial of services to those who fail to conform to the stereotype.

In the long term, what Elias (1993) has termed the 'hidden' wing of the victims' movement (as against the 'official' movement) will either wither away through lack of resources or will gain increased recognition because it provides services which are needed. There are some signs that both Victim Support and the statutory agencies are beginning to realise that the various victim support organisations have the potential to work together rather than in competition. Some Victim Support schemes have helped to set up Rape Crisis centres and train their volunteers; many local projects refer clients to one another; and the probation service has begun to engage with specialist victim agencies in some parts of the country. There is a growing recognition that victim support services designed for 'ideal' victims (Walklate 1989) fail to meet certain needs and that this can be remedied. Nevertheless, the various agencies have been forced into competing for resources when their respective services and campaigning activities ought to have been recognised as complementary.

Paradoxically, political and official priorities have hampered dialogue between the officially sponsored and the 'hidden' victims' movements. The imposition by central government of a particular model of victimisation and victim support, based upon individual remedies rather than recognising structural factors, is aimed at a closure of the debate. The hidden victims' movement has resisted this and has struggled, with some success, for greater visibility. In doing so it has contributed to the politicisation of victims' issues by broadening the range of political ideas and images of victims under debate. Government attempts to prevent this discussion from taking place by denying such groups funding and failing to consult representatives of the hidden movement were, of course, no less politically motivated.

The agencies involved in supporting victims have a dual role in caring for individuals and in highlighting the issues raised by their work. It is the degree of emphasis placed upon the public education function, and upon political agitation around victimisation, that distinguishes Victim Support from some of the other organisations. For the first twenty years of its existence, Victim Support went out of its way to avoid political controversy (while still, nevertheless, taking part in the political process, but largely behind the scenes). This strategy gained the organisation many friends in the Home Office and, doubtless, helped to secure its funding. It also prevented internal disagreements and helped to ensure the independence of the organisation, according to two of its founding members writing some years later.

They did go on to note, however, that the time might soon come when it would be appropriate to campaign more vocally and overtly on victims' behalf (Holtom and Raynor 1988). The strategy duly changed, albeit cautiously. For example, the national umbrella organisation began to associate itself with criticisms of government policy (notably in the case of proposed changes to the Criminal Injuries Compensation Scheme in 1995). Also, in 1995 it published a pamphlet which did not stop at setting out the existing rights of victims but went on to draw attention to many areas where legal and administrative reforms were needed – and, in doing so, the discourse of rights, rather than that of needs, was employed (Victim Support 1995). Local schemes did not always favour the campaigning role undertaken by national Victim Support and it may have had an adverse impact upon central government funding levels, so Victim Support remains cautious about engaging too explicitly in the political process (Kosh and Williams 1995; see also Chapter One).

For all the local victim organisations, the first priority is to support individual victims in need. They all collect information with a view to advising central and local government on the prevalence of victimisation:

while providing a confidential service and keeping few records of their contact with individuals, they also compile aggregate statistics in order to show that their services are needed. Most of them also publish case studies (with the permission of the people involved, whose identities are concealed) for use in fund-raising and, in some cases, campaigning. The central government funding of Victim Support, for example, is calculated partly on the basis of a formula which links staffing levels with the numbers of victims visited in their homes. Local authority contributions to agencies will also often depend upon evidence being provided of the level of demand for the service. Political pressures operate here too – for example, London Rape Crisis Centre was threatened with the withdrawal of its local authority funding in 1995 in a dispute over the nature of the advice being given to people who called its confidential telephone advice service. The London Borough Grants Committee proposed the appointment of an observer who would have listened to supposedly confidential telephone calls on behalf of the sponsoring councils, a suggestion which was withdrawn after the intervention of the British Association for Counselling and protests from other Rape Crisis centres around the country (Angela 1997). Funding agencies were proposing to compromise callers' confidentiality to ensure that the content of calls met with their approval, and this was ethically unacceptable to Rape Crisis and the BAC.

The agencies differ significantly in the extent to which they see themselves as having a campaigning role. Local Victim Support schemes largely leave this to their national office but smaller organisations, such as Rape Crisis centres, have only recently come together in a national federation which can intervene in national media debates, although they have been accustomed to intervening in local debates about the prevalence of violence against women and the best ways of dealing with it. They, along with Women's Aid, take part in local TV and radio programmes and raise issues in the press, as well as providing training for criminal justice and social services professionals (Ball 1994; Marchant 1993; Perry 1993; T. 1988). They have also been prominent in initiating local domestic violence forums, which bring together the agencies involved in responding to violence against women, to consider improved policies and practices (Hague, Malos and Dear 1996), although such initiatives have faltered in the face of funding difficulties and more urgent priorities in some areas and questions have been raised about their effectiveness (Hague 1997).

This insistence upon raising the broader issues which arise from their work with victims has resulted in pro-feminist victim agencies being labelled as strident and anti-men by many people working in the criminal justice system. This inevitably leads to a reluctance by some agencies and individuals to refer victims to them, to become involved in their management and to argue for state funding to help finance their activities. Such an image may also, at one time, have discouraged some victims from referring themselves for help. It has also further marginalised them: when the Parliamentary All-Party Penal Affairs Group (PAPPAG) last enquired into the question of victims' rights, for example, it consulted Victim Support, Mediation UK and the Zito Trust, but no women's organisations. This selectivity certainly reduced the breadth and quality of the resulting report (PAPPAG 1996).

The PAPPAG paper also ignored the question of racial harassment and violence, and the parliamentary group was not alone in leaving these matters out of consideration of victims' needs and rights. Just as the pro-feminist organisations have been pushed to the periphery of debates about victimisation, so have anti-racist groups campaigning at local level against racially motivated crime. Some racial harassment projects have received central and local government funding, at least on an experimental basis, but their existence is generally as hand-to-mouth as that of the women's groups. Where they become effective at representing and assisting victims, they are sometimes characterised as taking the law into their own hands – and seen as vigilante groups rather than self-help organisations. Clearly, the distinction between self-help and vigilantism depends upon where the person making the judgement stands. Victims of crime which is motivated by racial hatred need to be dealt with as sympathetically as possible and self-help groups have come into existence largely because this need was not being effectively met by existing agencies. They have shown that black-led organisations can and do provide an effective response (HWBSG 1993; Saini et al. 1997). Elsewhere, local authorities and community groups have set up successful projects in partnership (Sampson and Phillips 1995; Saulsbury and Bowling 1991). Such activities can help to change the climate in which complainants are often arrested when the police arrive because they are inaccurately perceived as the source of the trouble rather than as the victims (Strobl 1997).

As with sexual and 'domestic' violence, the problems of racial harassment and abuse have often been marginalised by the police and by Victim Support (which never even finds out about most offences if the police do not take them seriously enough to prosecute) (see Radford and Stanko 1991). Specialist projects have responded to the unmet need and, inevitably, their response has had not merely palliative but also political motivation. They have provided help for individual victims but they have also identified a need for community self-help and, in some cases, for action on a broader front. For example, Sampson and Phillips (1995) found that the housing department in an East End borough in London tended not to take complaints of racial harassment by its tenants seriously and continued to allocate Bengali families accommodation on an estate where it was not safe for them to live. When the local law centre initiated court proceedings to prevent a particular family from being sent there, the council changed its housing allocation policy. The researchers' study of repeated racial attacks on particular families, and the responses employed by other local councils, also led to policy changes. In the process the inter-agency project working to reduce racial attacks on the estate became very unpopular with local councillors who were involved in deciding on the future funding of the project, but significant improvements were achieved despite these tensions.

Such organisations demonstrate that support for individual victims can be combined effectively with campaigning for political change – but there is clearly a dilemma for workers in victim support agencies, whose main concern is relieving the distress of individual victims and who feel the need to maintain good relations with the police and other local authorities. This issue is considered further towards the end of this chapter and in Chapter Five.

The Citizen's and Victim's Charters and citizens' rights

Before considering the Victim's Charter, it is important to place it in the context of the then Prime Minister's Citizen's Charter Initiative. Citizens only have rights if they are aware of what these rights are, believe in the authenticity of such rights and have 'the skills needed to exercise them' (Marshall 1975, p.207).

The Citizen's Charter Initiative was an attempt to bring about the first two of these conditions, but it was flawed in a number of ways. For one thing, public awareness and even the availability of the various charters is poor. Academic researchers have had difficulty in getting hold of copies of some of them (Tritter 1994), which suggests that members of the public are unlikely to find it easy to identify and claim the rights set out in such documents.

While the Citizen's Charter and the charter documents issued subsequently by individual government departments, privatised utilities and quangos acknowledged and aimed to protect citizens' rights, they rarely announced the creation of any new ones (Tritter 1994). Where the charters did set out people's rights, this was done wholly in terms of *individual* rights and no reference was made to collective methods of claiming citizenship rights. The government recognised the potential for struggles over citizenship rights and, by means of the charter initiative, sought to institutionalise a largely individualised and bureaucratic conception of citizenship.

In this way some of the existing public hostility towards welfare bureaucracies was redirected away from the national politicians who make the laws and set the budgets which govern the distribution of welfare at a local level and towards the agencies providing those services locally. Many of the charters (including the Victim's Charter) place a heavy emphasis upon how to complain about local services.

By framing the discourse of citizenship in terms of individual consumer rights rather than acknowledging the possibility of collective action in the pursuit of citizens' rights, the government was able to advance a number of its own political ends in the name of improving the lot of the citizen.

These processes are illustrated by the Victim's Charter (Home Office 1990, 1996) and each of the general arguments above will now be considered specifically in respect of victims' rights.

Although the Victim's Charter is available on demand from Victim Support schemes, police stations and the Home Office, its existence and purpose are not widely known outside these agencies. The 1996 version of the charter is a twenty-page pamphlet and is too bulky to be distributed to all victims of reported crime. It is not written in very accessible language and it acknowledges its own limitations by placing considerable emphasis on how to make complaints about criminal justice agencies and on where to obtain fuller information. Instead of using copies of the Victim's Charter itself, the police in most areas send out brief explanatory leaflets referring to the services available to victims. (The charter contains a lengthy list of other leaflets and a selection of addresses to contact but is not a self-contained statement of services or rights.) Many local Victim Support schemes also prefer to use their own nationally and locally prepared materials, even though they have access to free supplies of the charter. It is, therefore, markedly unsuccessful as an attempt to publicise victims' existing rights and encourage people to claim such entitlements.

In any event, the original version of the Victim's Charter did not create any new rights or new ways of claiming existing rights and the emphasis was firmly upon individual rather than collective action. The 1990 edition simply set out the progress to date on improving the position of victims within the criminal justice system, some 'guiding principles' on the treatment of victims and 'a checklist of questions' for criminal justice agencies to consider. Thus although the charter had obvious implications for the police, prosecution, probation and court services, any action was left to their discretion.

It made reference to Victim Support schemes but not to other sources of help, even in the sections referring specifically to victims of murder, rape and domestic violence where specialist (but 'hidden') victim support agencies exist. There was no reference at all to racial harassment and violence. In such cases the hidden victim support organisations could undoubtedly help, but their approach is collective as well as individual. They aim to educate the public about the sources and consequences of violence, particularly male violence and racially motivated crime, as well as helping individual victims, and they provide a focus for collective action on these issues. As such, their existence is ignored in official publications such as the Victim's Charter, which sought to publicise the government's achievements rather than those of a potentially oppositional victims' movement.

The Victim's Charter did, however, draw attention to a number of areas where government policy was not being implemented. This was done very discreetly but the document contained several signals to criminal justice agencies that change was overdue. For example, the section on 'reporting the crime' consists of six sentences all beginning 'The police should…' and all referring to ways of treating victims which, while good practice, were not in place in many police services (Home Office 1990). Similarly, one of the 'checklist of questions' for magistrates' courts was: 'Has s. 104 of the Criminal Justice Act 1988 (compensation orders) led to markedly more orders being made? Are reasons recorded when an order is not made?' (Home Office 1990, p.25).

Again, the section of the main charter relating to compensation reiterated that, 'When an offender is convicted, the court must always consider ordering him [sic] to pay some compensation to his [sic] victim' (Home Office 1990, p.18). This is a reference to the legal requirement that courts give reasons when not ordering compensation in cases where a criminal offence has an individual victim. In practice, it was not being implemented and the reminder that courts should record their reasons was presumably intended to ensure that the law would in future be applied as intended by Parliament (see Chapter One).

Academic observers and those within Victim Support were critical of the failure of the Victim's Charter to create new rights (Cavadino and Dignan 1990; Fenwick 1995; Victim Support 1990, 1995).[1] Evidence soon became available, however, of a will within the Home Office to ensure that changes were made and that the creation of some limited, but enforceable, rights was part of the strategy to achieve this. In the period between the publication of the first edition and the relaunch of the Victim's Charter in 1996, various criminal justice agencies were given new responsibilities towards victims and a variety of enforcement mechanisms was put in place (see Chapter Five).

Taking the probation service as an example, the 1990 Charter created an expectation that release plans in respect of life-sentence prisoners would in future be 'prepared with due regard to the victim's (or the victim's family's) wishes and interests' (Home Office 1990, p.25). This was the subject of circular instructions in 1994 and 1995 and reference was made to the requirement to undertake such work in the 1995 National Standards for the supervision of prisoners before and after their release. By the time the 1996 Victim's Charter was published, with its statement that 'The probation service will take your concerns into account when making their plans' (Home Office 1996, p.12), structures were in place to ensure that victims' voices were indeed heard as part of the process of planning for the release of the most serious offenders from prison.

Another tentative suggestion in the 1990 Victim's Charter was that consideration should be given to victims' interests in all aspects of the work of the probation service. Again, circular instructions and National Standards were used as an enforcement mechanism and policy and practice changed accordingly (albeit inconsistently and slowly – see Nettleton, Walklate and Williams 1997). In particular, probation reports began to include much fuller discussion of the damage suffered by victims of the crimes committed by offenders who were the subjects of the reports than in the past. Information

---

1   Victim Support did not explicitly criticise the Victim's Charter in its 1995 pamphlet
     but set out victims' existing rights alongside problems which remained to be dealt
     with.

about victims' perspectives on crime came to be used more often in individual supervision and group work with offenders. Some probation services appointed specialist staff to work with victims and liaise with victims' organisations. Most published new policy documents about their responsibilities towards victims and reviewed their existing procedures and practices.

While it may still be true to say that the Victim's Charter created no new, enforceable, legal rights, it did influence the policy and practice of criminal justice agencies in significant ways, and this led to improvements in the position of victims. However, these all occurred in the context of the rights of the individual victim and there was no official encouragement of the emerging victims' movement or of any kind of collective response to criminal victimisation. The Victim's Charter frames all its statements about victims' entitlements in terms of the victim as a consumer of services. This language of consumer standards (the reference to 'rights' in the subtitle of the 1990 version is replaced by 'service standards' in the 1996 version) conceals a number of political assumptions and motives on the part of the then government.

First, framing 'service standards' in terms of what 'you can expect', as the 1996 Victim's Charter does, is part of an attempt to shift any blame for the inadequacy of provision for victims onto the local services responsible for providing them and to devolve difficult decisions about priorities to the local level. It thus serves to draw attention away from the fact that these services are underfunded and subject to competing, even contradictory, requirements imposed by central government. The Victim's Charter creates expectations among victims of crime (in so far as they are aware of its provisions) but there is no corresponding offender's charter – which makes it easier for criminal justice services to justify abandoning previous provisions for work with offenders in order to fund victims' services. This may be an entirely proper way of distributing scarce resources but it has gone largely undebated and may lead to a neglect of efforts to protect potential victims by working towards the rehabilitation of offenders. Local agencies have had to make decisions on priorities based upon their perceptions of the relative popularity of, and level of, political support for particular groups of service users.

Inevitably, victims of crime will be a higher priority than offenders, although the two groups overlap in reality and the interests of victims may be best served in practice by helping offenders to change their behaviour and attitudes. The irony of placing such responsibilities upon the probation service, whose prime responsibility remains the supervision of offenders, has not been lost upon the agencies concerned – but the cost of setting up a separate statutory service to work with victims was, no doubt, prohibitive (Kosh and Williams 1995; Williams 1996).

It could be argued that the changes are part of a wider project of imposing discipline upon public sector agencies, using the Charter Initiative as a tool. Many of the agencies concerned are unpopular, for a whole variety of reasons, not least those arising from spending constraints and the consequent rationing of services, but probation also has the stigma of being perceived as a service for offenders. Without significantly increased spending, the Victim's Charter offers a method of holding criminal justice agencies accountable to central government priorities and leaves individual victims to police the process by making complaints. The charter thus places a heavy emphasis upon how to complain about the police, the prosecution service, probation, the courts, Victim Support and the Criminal Injuries Compensation Authority.

Central government will be able to decide whether and how to respond to any increase in complaints and may choose to use such a trend as a reason to reform criminal justice agencies in line with its existing priorities. For example, if the semi-independent Probation Inspectorate were to draw attention to inadequacies in the probation service's work with victims of crime, this might form part of a case for even greater central government direction of its work (a trend which has increased rapidly since the mid-1980s: see Drakeford and Vanstone 1996; Williams 1996). If the Police Complaints Authority were to note an increase in complaints about police insensitivity towards victims, this might be used as an argument for increasing the pace of the programme of civilianisation of traditional police functions. The potential for political manipulation is considerable and it was probably intentionally built into the Charter Initiative.

On a more mundane level, the public concern about the inadequacy of service provision is largely contained by the charters at a local and bureaucratic level – complainants are always expected to exhaust local procedures before approaching higher authorities. On the one hand, the government is using the Victim's Charter to encourage people to complain, but, on the other, it largely insulates itself from hearing about the social and structural issues giving rise to the complaints. Nowhere is it suggested that people use the political process to voice grievances: the possibility of taking issues up with councillors or members of parliament is never mentioned in the charter, let alone the possibility of involving victims' organisations or other advocacy groups in 'class actions'. Thus welfare and criminal justice bureaucracies can be regulated without any new mechanisms being created to enforce what few rights citizens have in this area.

Finally, the Victim's Charter has a role in helping to keep any emergent social movement of victims of crime under control. It continues the government's policy of marginalising pro-feminist, anti-racist and single-issue self-help victims' organisations by the simple expedient of ignoring their existence. It is remarkable that such a document should contain a reference to the NSPCC but none to Women's Aid refuges. The only plausible explanation for such selectivity is that it avoids putting victims in touch with support agencies which have valuable services to offer because they also provide opportunities for victims to campaign about the causes of criminal victimisation and put forward political demands. More subtly, by individualising the experience of victimisation and reducing it to a list of what 'you can expect' from criminal justice agencies, it distracts attention from the possibility that there might be structural problems underlying crime and that collective action might be an effective method of response (Williams 1997). This issue is discussed further in Chapter Six.

The picture is a complex one and it is too simplistic to argue that the Victim's Charter was merely a cynical device which was not backed by any intention to improve the position of victims of crime. Many agencies and individuals have influenced the policy changes described above but the publication of the two versions of the Victim's Charter undoubtedly strengthened the hand of those who saw a need for change. Subsequent changes amount to a significant reorientation of the criminal justice system in England and Wales which is intended to give victims' interests greater priority, although the system remains largely offender-focused. For example, reparation orders made under the provisions of the 1998 *Crime and Disorder Act* will require young offenders to make direct recompense to victims, where this is acceptable to them, and victims will be consulted before decisions are made. The same Act increases the restrictions which can be imposed upon sexual offenders, in the name of protecting past and potential victims, although it remains to be seen how effective this will prove to be.

Victims set against offenders

Although there is evidence that many victims of crime are themselves ex-offenders (Peelo *et al.* 1992; Widom 1991), it is a common mistake to assume that the two groups are completely distinct from one another. An adversarial criminal justice system sets the offender's advocate (the defence) against the victim's (or the state's) representative in the form of the prosecution lawyer. This model of criminal justice creates a false dichotomy between the interests of victims and those of offenders, which has led to polarised discussion and policy making based on an assumption that the interests of victims and those of offenders are always diametrically and automatically opposed.

Simplistic approaches to policy making in relation to victims of crime, therefore, often lead to counter-productive measures and to invidious choices being made between offender and victim services. Obvious examples include the American 'war on drugs', which has criminalised hundreds of thousands of people without offering them rehabilitative opportunities or doing anything to help their victims when they offend and reoffend (Elias 1993). The ultimate logic of this policy was 'three strikes and you're out' sentencing, which has led to the incarceration of many thousands of people, including some relatively minor offenders, for 'life' sentences. When released, these prisoners are likely to have become hardened and embittered and will quickly reoffend. It is difficult to see how this helps their actual or potential future victims.

Similarly, the imprisonment of young and minor offenders does little to assist their victims, who, in many (or even most) cases, might prefer reassurance, an apology, reparative measures and compensation (Hough and Mayhew 1983; Koffman 1996; Reeves and Wright 1995). To achieve this, radical changes would need to be made to most western criminal justice systems. Experiments in restorative justice have been under way for some years and there are encouraging signs that ways can be found of placing the victim at the centre of the sentencing process without creating pressure on victims to make actual sentencing decisions (Lupton 1998; Marsh and Crow 1998). It is very important that victims are not put under this kind of stress because it is quite clear that most do not welcome involvement in sentencing as such (Morris, Maxwell and Robertson 1993; Reeves and Wright 1995). What they generally do want is to be consulted and to receive information about the offender, the sentence and subsequent release plans in cases where offenders are imprisoned. Where they also want to receive a direct or indirect apology, or to meet the offender and express their feelings, this can be arranged in criminal justice systems which are sufficiently flexible (Hudson and Galaway 1996).

Where the Victim's Charter is concerned, a number of further examples of the process of changing the system at the expense of offenders' interests and in the name of victims, without necessarily improving the situation of victims, come to mind.

When the charter was first published, there was no consultation with criminal justice agencies about its detail or implementation. In the case of the probation service this meant that new services had to be provided without any additional resources or very much advance planning. One implication, in some areas, was that bail information schemes for suspected offenders were closed down (these investigate the case for releasing certain offenders on bail after they are remanded in custody by magistrates' courts, usually because the court lacks the information it needs to make a decision to release them on bail).

Another concern was that probation staff who (in the early days) had not had the opportunity to receive any specialist training were suddenly required to contact victims to make enquiries in connection with the possible release of the prisoners who had offended against them and were being considered for release at the end of life sentences. Perhaps not surprisingly, such enquiries were not always made with sufficient tact or sensitivity. In many cases victims or surviving family members were contacted 'out of the blue', ten, twelve or even more years after the original offence, by probation officers under pressure to provide reports to the prison and parole authorities at short notice. As one probation officer said, such hurried interviews were 'too hurtful... you're not there to support the victim when they need it and you're not there to pick up the pieces afterwards. You need a lot of support in place before you plough in with your big feet as I did' (Kosh and Williams 1995, p.21).

Such support was not available in this case, and there were probably many others like it. This was clearly not in the victims' best interests, but probation officers had to follow a policy ostensibly aimed at conferring new rights upon victims and this was the consequence. Practice has since greatly improved and a training programme has been instituted, but the mistakes need never have been made in the first place and the responsibility for them lies with the politicians rather than the practitioners who tried to make sense of the political decisions (see Nettleton, Walklate and Williams 1997).

Similarly, the 1995 National Standards for the Supervision of Offenders introduced a new requirement (reiterated in the 1996 Victim's Charter) that probation staff should contact the victims of serious crimes within two months of sentence being passed in cases where the offender received a prison sentence. Again, this provision was an unexpected extension of the earlier arrangements in respect of lifers and the probation response varied considerably. In some areas it was possible to implement it immediately; in other places the work remained undone for a further two years or more. Indeed, the Home Office was forced to issue a departmental circular in 1997 to find out the extent to which it was being implemented: no evaluative research had been arranged. Meanwhile, prisoners were being refused release because such enquiries had not been made of victims, and victims were receiving different treatment depending on where they happened to live. When the offender or the victim had moved house since the offence, more than one probation area could become involved and the inconsistencies in practice became even more apparent (Nettleton, Walklate and Williams 1997).

There was considerable reluctance on the part of the Home Office in the mid-1990s to plan ahead or to consult the organisations involved in the delivery of services to victims. This was, perhaps, partly due to the unpopularity both of the then government and its Home Secretary, who was anxious to take initiatives which would improve his political position but deeply distrusted the agencies which would have to deliver the services involved. It is extremely unfortunate that victim policy has been subject to such political game-playing – and this is by no means confined to the UK, as Robert Elias' work on the political manipulation of victims in the USA shows (Elias 1993).

A more balanced approach to policy on victims of crime would recognise the links and overlaps between offending and victimisation and would seek to reconcile conflicts between the two groups rather than highlighting them for political effect. Major changes to victim services would be phased in gradually, rather than being suddenly announced at press conferences (or at political party and police trade union conferences).

In the longer term a re-examination of the inquisitorial (some say gladiatorial) basis of most western criminal justice systems is needed, and this work has begun in several countries. As restorative approaches to criminal justice gain credibility and respect, it will, perhaps, become more difficult to manipulate the criminal justice system for political effect. Part of the problem at present is that victims have no legitimate official role in many criminal justice systems. When their part in decision making has been institutionalised (as, for example, in New Zealand's youth justice system), power can be transferred from the central state to the local community and to victims themselves. Then, local people begin to develop a sense of ownership of the decision-making process (McElrea 1996). It will be interesting to see whether experiments with such a model of justice in England have a similar effect (Wright 1996).

Managing the tension between individual and social change

Agencies working with victims should not feel constrained by the nature of their funding arrangements from highlighting problematic aspects of the working of the criminal justice system. In practice, however, groups like Victim Support are acutely aware that they depend heavily upon central government funding. They have, therefore, tended to avoid controversy, both for this reason and because of a feeling that it would have a divisive effect on staff and volunteers (Holtom and Raynor 1988; Reeves and Wright 1995). Other victim agencies do manage this tension successfully, but they are not as generously funded as Victim Support in the first place and most receive no central government financial support at all.

Because it covers a wide range of victims and draws its volunteers from a variety of backgrounds (Aye Maung 1993), Victim Support mostly confines itself to making fairly general comments about criminal justice policy, but also commissions and publishes research on the special needs and rights of victims in general and on the victims of particular types of crime. Local schemes avoid political involvement (and are required by the organisation to do so) but the national office has a lobbying role and increasingly intervenes in political discussions about victim issues.

Single-issue organisations can find it much easier to reach agreement about the political positions they should adopt. Victim Support volunteers espouse a variety of explanations of crime and victimisation, whereas people involved in Women's Aid and Rape Crisis generally adopt a feminist approach to understanding male violence (Mullender 1996; Radford and Stanko 1991; T. 1988; Wilson 1996). Such groups combine caring for victims with an educational role and they tend to be comfortable with the idea of political campaigning as part of that mission. Other victim agencies, too, can make political statements secure in the knowledge that their members will mostly agree with them because it was shared indignation about the treatment received from the criminal justice system that motivated them to come together in the first place. One example is the position that Support After Murder and Manslaughter takes on the life sentence: few of its members disagree with SAMM's public position that 'life' should always mean that murderers remain in prison for the rest of their lives. Similarly, the American group Mothers Against Drunk Drivers has campaigned for stronger legal penalties against drunken driving and has made it known that its members monitor particular judges' sentencing decisions with a view to publicising any examples of undue lenience (Elias 1993).

Not all political campaigning by victims' groups involves calls for harsher sentencing, however. Victim Support, for example, has frequently made clear that there is no benefit for victims in removing the rights of those accused of crime:

> the retributive basis of the system... necessitates extensive safeguards for defendants, and gave rise to the dictum that it is better to acquit ninety-nine guilty men than to convict one innocent – but the victim is conscious that both types of miscarriage of justice leave the real perpetrator at large. (Reeves and Wright 1995, p.80)

In a similar spirit, projects working to prevent violence against women, and to ensure that it is taken seriously when it occurs, do not necessarily advocate the more frequent use of imprisonment. They argue that it should be reserved for the most serious cases, recognising that prison is unlikely to improve violent men's attitudes whereas some community sentences can do so (Wilson 1996).

In the UK the victims' movement has avoided becoming associated with those campaigning for stronger law enforcement. In the USA the two issues have become intertwined and, to some extent, confused. In Canada a balance has been struck with a modified version of the American concept of zero tolerance: 'domestic' violence is taken seriously, and routinely dealt with as a criminal matter, but offenders are increasingly given treatment- rather than punishment-orientated sentences because this has been shown to be the most effective way of preventing reoffending. This approach is based upon a belief that 'rigorous prosecution should be pursued, but not at the expense of the victim' (Ursel 1998, p.77).

In many cases victims' organisations are well placed to monitor the performance of other criminal justice agencies and to ensure that action is taken if victims' interests are neglected. Local Victim Support schemes in England and Wales bring representatives of the police, probation and crown prosecution services (and, sometimes, individual magistrates) together on their committees and this improves the awareness of these staff of the impact of the system upon victims. From the beginning, local schemes have been required to seek representation of the local statutory agencies on their committees. When things do go wrong, Victim Support co-ordinators will help individuals to make complaints but, more often, they contact the offending agency to point out deficiencies in services, often through the existing contact with a member of the scheme's committee. Local groups also ensure that the national Victim Support office is well-informed about any legal and administrative changes arising from groups' involvement with local individuals which need to be made (Reeves and Wright 1995).

The more radical groups tend to have difficult relationships with criminal justice agencies, particularly the police, because they are in frequent contact with service users who report finding police officers prejudiced and oppressive, and experience this themselves as well. They also insist on respecting service users' right to confidentiality and police officers investigating allegations sometimes find this difficult to understand (T. 1988). Nevertheless, Rape Crisis centres and Women's Aid refuges are often involved in police training: 'Mostly, we manage to remain polite to the arrogant and the authoritarian, whether during these talks, or when providing support to women who are reporting rape, or when a police officer decides it would be a "good idea" for a woman to be referred to us' (T. 1988, p.63).

There are mutual benefits to be had from improving communication in this way. Small, underfunded agencies can charge fees for providing training and use the opportunity to put their message over and encourage reflection about prevailing attitudes. The formal criminal justice agencies can take the opportunity to improve staff awareness of victim issues and enhance public relations. Victims themselves can only benefit from such an exchange as long as it is constructive, rather than unduly abrasive. In some areas the police report much-improved relationships with the self-help agencies. There are bound to be times, however, when conflict is necessary and constructive: the arrogant, authoritarian and sexist treatment of women Rape Crisis workers and service users described by Anna T. is simply unacceptable and has to be confronted.

Volunteers' views about the appropriateness of political interventions by victims' agencies vary, as one might expect. Little research evidence exists on volunteers' attitudes. Mawby and Gill (1987) found Victim Support volunteers in the south-west of England similar, in a number of ways, to special constables: members of both groups tended to offer their services partly out of a commitment to upholding law and order in a society where crime was seen as a major problem. VS volunteers tended to have a very positive view of the police but 'no dramatic or distinctive wish for harsher sentences' (Mawby and Gill 1987, p.214). The authors attributed this largely to the way in which Victim Support schemes were structured, with substantial police involvement and a strong discouragement of political involvement by local schemes. Victim Support volunteers rarely became involved because of their own direct experience of victimisation and because older, middle-class women were over-represented in their ranks (findings replicated by Aye Maung in 1993). In contrast, personal experience of victimisation is a common motivating factor among Rape Crisis and Women's Aid volunteers (who are all female but not disproportionately middle class). Those volunteers who work with the feminist groups bring an understanding of the personal as political, whether or not they have themselves experienced male violence, and these organisations generally train their volunteers in styles of counselling which encourage gradual, user-led approaches.

Kosh and Williams (1995) found that Victim Support scheme co-ordinators and committee members did not all welcome the level of political activity of the national organisation and some were critical of its closeness to the Home Office and its willingness to become identified with new areas of work which fitted in with Home Office priorities but not necessarily with those of local schemes. There were long-serving volunteers who identified a process of professionalisation and co-option which they did not welcome: as one said, 'The trouble with Victim Support, [is that] national office has become like everything else, a huge pressure group... We started out as being strictly a-religious, apolitical, a-everything...' (quoted in Kosh and Williams 1995, p.18).

On the other hand, some Victim Support volunteers who have undertaken advanced training in order to work with particular groups such as rape survivors feel that it is entirely appropriate for the national organisation to lobby for legal and procedural changes.

Volunteers in the single-issue victims' groups are even more inclined to support the idea of political activism to improve the treatment of victims. Members of Rape Crisis, for example, are often involved in various kinds of educational and campaigning work at local level, whether it takes the form of police training or radio interviews on International Women's Day. Although very circumspect about commenting on individual cases, they take every opportunity to raise issues relating to the law on rape. Their one-to-one work also proceeds from a belief in the re-empowerment of women who have been oppressed. As one activist put it: 'To me, citizenship is political: you take responsibility for what goes on in your community, you don't just sit whingeing, you do something about it. The personal is political' (group interview with Rape Crisis volunteers).

This raises a number of issues, including the view of citizenship which underlies different models of practice with victims. The Victim's Charter characterises victims primarily as passive consumers of services while the Rape Crisis worker quoted above sees her involvement with survivors – including the educational work with the wider community – as a legitimate political responsibility. While it would be unduly conspiratorial to suggest that the Victim's Charter was specifically designed to co-opt victims' organisations, it has undoubtedly had the effect of encouraging compliance by voluntary agencies which seek central government funding with the establishment view of their role. The feminist-inspired organisations have been marginalised at the expense of the more conciliatory Victim Support precisely because they do remain committed to a political conception of victimisation.

The need to provide appropriate support has constantly to be balanced with the wider picture, and poorly-resourced organisations face particularly difficult choices here. These are illustrated in the case studies in Chapter Five.

Who Helps Victims?

As we have seen, a wide range of organisations exists to meet victims' needs and to argue for their rights. Throughout this book examples have been drawn from the work of these different agencies. This chapter looks at some voluntary groups in more detail, including Victim Support schemes, Rape Crisis centres, Women's Aid refuges and Support After Murder and Manslaughter groups. Case studies are used to illustrate good practice and the differences of approach between the various organisations. The responsibilities of statutory organisations such as the police, probation and crown prosecution services are also considered. The chapter goes on to describe the ways in which the different groups work together and to suggest possible approaches to improving relationships between them – an issue considered further in Chapter Six.

Not surprisingly, there are overlaps between the work of victim support agencies in the UK but, in some cases, they have collaborated successfully for years, referring clients to each other and undertaking joint volunteer training. At times, however, there are also conflicts between the different groups which work with victims of crime.

For example, Victim Support receives substantial government funding and other organisations doing similar work get none. Where there is an overlapping group of service users, such as women subjected to domestic violence, there are sometimes tensions at a local level when Victim Support refers people who need long-term help to Women's Aid, which may be considerably less well resourced to meet the identified need. Similar considerations apply to women needing help in the aftermath of rape or childhood sexual abuse. In many areas such problems have been overcome by inter-agency negotiation, but decisions made at the centre do not always make this easy.

There may also be instances in which there are more profound differences between the various voluntary sector agencies, arising from their different understandings of what responses are required to criminal victimisation. Whereas a local racial harassment project might wish to use the evidence it collects about problems in a particular area arising from the activities of racist individuals or groups to put pressure on the local authority to change housing allocation policy or to argue for protection for black tenants, this partly political response to victims would be unacceptable to some victim support agencies – it would be seen as likely to compromise their political neutrality and their relationship with local authorities. Again, the existence of a range of provisions may be no bad thing if it means that victims' needs can be met in one of a variety of ways, but there are obvious problems if the various approaches lead to conflict between potentially competing victims' organisations.

A series of case studies will now be used to illustrate some of these issues more fully.

Victim Support

Victim Support is a long-established voluntary organisation with over 16,000 volunteers and almost 900 paid staff (Victim Support 1997). Most of its local schemes have full-time staff, although in some rural areas they are run by voluntary co-ordinators. Details of victims of crime are received regularly from the police, as well as some self-referrals. A volunteer is allocated to priority cases within a few days and makes an approach either by telephone or by visiting. A letter from the scheme's office is generally sent in advance, particularly where more serious offences are involved, and women reporting rape or sexual assaults are always seen by female volunteers. The funding formula whereby Victim Support receives central government finance is calculated according to the number of visits made to crime victims in their homes, which gives local scheme co-ordinators an incentive to encourage such home visits and the practice of 'cold calling' where no telephone number is known. Those victims who require further assistance may be visited more than once, but the majority of referrals are dealt with after one or two contacts and voluntary visitors are not trained as counsellors. However, some specialist volunteers (who receive additional training) do work with victims of more serious offences for a longer time, in some cases over a period of years.

As a large national organisation with an established relationship with the Home Office and other government departments, Victim Support has some political influence. It has frequently drawn attention to new areas of need, funding and evaluating pilot schemes and demonstration projects to provide evidence. A recent example is Witness Support: local Victim Support schemes had noted that victims frequently had unwelcome and distressing encounters with the accused when they went to court to give evidence and that court officials failed to provide the information about the criminal process and the progress of their own case that such witnesses needed. An experimental project aimed at meeting these needs was a demonstrable success and the campaign began to obtain central government funding for nationwide coverage by Witness Support schemes, an aim achieved in respect of Crown Courts in England and Wales by 1996. The argument for extending the provision of support for witnesses to magistrates' courts is now being put by Victim Support's national office and by local Witness Support schemes.

This process of demonstrating a need and then arguing for the necessary resources to be allocated has been repeated a number of times over the years, and Victim Support has grown correspondingly. By concentrating on victims' needs, VS has been able to achieve considerable improvements in service provision and in official attitudes towards victims. It has also avoided growing so fast that the quality of its services suffered: Witness Support, for example, was set up with its own local committee structures and volunteers and, although identifiably part of VS, it nevertheless has its own administration and sources of income. While other, smaller initiatives were undertaken as part of local VS schemes, they were organised in ways which facilitated a degree of autonomy, as in the case of specialist provision for work with sexually abused women and the survivors of murder victims. Specialist volunteers were thus recruited and supported without taking too many resources away from the day-to-day work of schemes.

It might be argued that Victim Support has paid a high price for this careful strategy of first demonstrating and then meeting need: although resources have been forthcoming from central government, the organisation has, perhaps, become over-dependent upon this income and lost some of its freedom to criticise government policy. Other organisations are prepared to do so but they forfeit official funding by their critical stance. Although VS has always advocated remaining politically neutral, there have been times when it has spoken out against Home Office policy – as when a Conservative Home Secretary attempted to cut the cost of the criminal injuries compensation scheme (see Chapter Two) by reducing payments to victims and simplifying the process of assessing compensation levels.

While undoubtedly at the 'respectable' end of the spectrum of victims' organisations, Victim Support has been very effective in raising public and political consciousness of victims' issues without undertaking much overtly political campaigning. It would be an unwise Home Secretary who ignored the issues raised by VS, but the relationship between VS and the Home Office has generally been a cordial one.

Case study

The following case study is based on one described by Victim Support in its report of a research project on rape and the criminal justice system (Victim Support 1996a).

> Jenny was raped, and reported the crime to the police the following day. She found the medical examination 'horrendous. If I had known about that before, I wouldn't have gone through with it.' Her examination, by a male doctor, took place in a police station, rather than a specialist rape examination suite, and she was not told that she could be seen by a woman doctor if she wished. Apart from this, she was full of praise for the way the police dealt with her case: the investigating officer kept her informed and phoned a number of times to check that she was alright. The defendant was granted bail (a decision she only found out about by reading a report in the local press) and Jenny found it very difficult to leave her house before the case came to court, knowing that she might see or be approached by him. She told the police about her concerns but there seemed to be very little that they could do.
>
> The police told her about Victim Support and Jenny contacted her local scheme at an early stage. A volunteer took her around an empty court before the trial, arranged a private room for her to wait in and supported her when the case was postponed three times. She also prepared Jenny for the possibility that the defendant might not be convicted. The man denied the offence when the case eventually came to court and Jenny was cross-examined by his barrister at length. The defendant was found 'not guilty'.
>
> Jenny felt that she was treated very badly by the courts and that justice had not been done in her case. She considered taking civil action against the accused but, after discussion with the Victim Support

volunteer, decided that this would merely prolong her suffering: 'I thought hard about it, but it had all gone on too long. I feel as if I have to put it all behind me. Even though it was two years ago, some days it feels like it was just yesterday.' (Victim Support 1996a, p.33)

In this case Victim Support has clearly been a great help to Jenny and the use of her case in a report of research on the way in which women are treated by the criminal justice system is part of an attempt to achieve changes which will help future defendants. One of the cases reported by Victim Support has been summarised here in order to illustrate the differences of approach by the organisations supporting people reporting rapes and the reader may wish to compare the case study above, and those in Chapter Three, with the one in the following section.

It is clear from the case study above that witnesses and complainants in rape cases may feel that they have been treated badly by the system (and that even where they feel they were treated well, improvements could be made). For example, local police practice was open to criticism on a number of grounds. Jenny was not kept informed, either about the court's decision to bail the defendant or about the availability of female police surgeons. Jenny was not offered protection, or even reassurance, when she expressed her fear of further contact with the defendant, although the police in some areas have developed specialist witness services to support vulnerable witnesses and prevent intimidation (see below). Victim Support schemes have a police representative sitting on their committees, but there is no mention in the case study of this link being used to take up the issues arising from the treatment of Jenny's case. It might be argued that, in this case, Victim Support concentrated on Jenny's needs as an individual – and gave her a good, personal, caring service – but that this was at the expense of some of the wider issues raised by her case. However, these can only be taken up where the person concerned wishes this to happen, and Jenny clearly wanted to get on with her life and put the attack behind her.

Rape Crisis

Rape Crisis has about fifty local groups, although the numbers fluctuate as a result of insecure funding arrangements. Groups have an average of a dozen volunteers and one or two paid staff (often part-time). Parts of the country are not adequately covered by the existing network of local Rape Crisis centres: at the time of writing, these include West Wales, Lincolnshire and Cornwall. Nevertheless, nearly 50,000 women contacted the centres for assistance in the year 1996/97, of whom only 7 per cent had reported the incident concerned to the police. Centres are linked by a national federation, whose values statement includes the recognition that sexual violence 'is an act of male aggression and power' and that 'women and girls have the right and essential ability to take control of their lives' as well as a right to the information and support they need to do so. It also recognises the importance of a feminist perspective and of 'the safety of women-only support' (RCF, undated).

This explicit political stance places Rape Crisis firmly in Elias' 'hidden' victims' movement, although it is a large and active organisation. Much of its work goes on, as it were, behind the scenes: its staff and volunteers avoid commenting on individual cases and find it hard to obtain publicity for the less newsworthy day-to-day issues like the need for adequate funding.

The main sources of funding for Rape Crisis' work are local authorities and local health trusts, and national and local charities. Some national funding has been received through the Opportunities for Volunteering fund and, in recent years, from the National Lottery. While the national federation argues for long-term funding through the Home Office on the same basis as the regular grant given to Victim Support, this has so far failed to come to fruition (Murray 1998). Given the explicit political stance taken by the Rape Crisis Federation, and the discussion of the politics of victim support funding in Chapter Four, this is, perhaps, not unduly surprising. National government distinguishes between the 'respectable' and relatively uncontroversial work of Victim Support and the more contentious and challenging approach of Rape Crisis. Despite the evident need for its services, Rape Crisis does not command mainstream political support, at least at the national level. Local authorities and health trusts show more signs of valuing its work for people in their areas.

Case study

> Emma was repeatedly raped by her stepfather from the age of eleven until leaving home. After seeing a TV programme about childhood sex abuse, she made a note of the telephone number given for the Rape Crisis Federation. It took her some time but she eventually decided to phone the centre nearest to her home. Emma was then involved in several months of counselling provided by the local Rape Crisis centre, which she found difficult but helpful. Her counsellor, Shauna, likened the process to peeling a large onion: gathering the courage to peel off

another layer can take weeks, and the peeling process was by no means easy or comfortable. After four months, Emma began to feel that she should consider reporting her stepfather to the police, not least in order to protect her six-year-old sister from abuse. Shauna encouraged her to consider the pros and cons and suggested that if the first priority was protecting the child, it would also be advisable to talk to the social services department or the NSPCC.

It took several more months before Emma felt strong enough to take this step and she began by writing an account of her experiences at the hands of her stepfather, which was discussed at a number of her appointments with Shauna. Shauna agreed to accompany her when an appointment was eventually made with the NSPCC. They agreed to mount an investigation without disclosing the source of their information. By that time, Emma had moved home and had decided not to disclose her new address to her family.

The aim of protecting the young girl was achieved and Emma decided not to involve the police. She continued to see Shauna regularly for some months and then their contact gradually tailed off, although she found it helpful to know that she could re-establish it whenever she might need to do so.

Rape Crisis centres train their staff and volunteers in non-directive counselling techniques and, in many cases, support women for long periods of time. The healing process takes priority over everything else and only a small minority of those disclosing rape or abuse decide to go to the police.

When a client does choose to involve the authorities, she receives full support throughout the process from her counsellor, who prepares her for the court process where appropriate. Some clients are accompanied during police interviews and court cases, and Rape Crisis centres have substantial accumulated experience of supporting women through the criminal justice process and, where necessary, of challenging the official agencies to provide appropriate services. They respect clients' confidentiality fully and there is no question of reporting allegations to the authorities in cases where clients object. In the case study there was evidence of an immediate threat to the welfare of a child and the client was encouraged and supported in taking appropriate action. Had she decided to take no action, this decision would have been respected, although the counsellor might have returned to the issue as her client gained strength and confidence in order to try and ensure that a child at risk received protection. Women's self-esteem can be all but destroyed as a result of abuse and the recovery process can be lengthy. Support, therefore, often needs to be provided over a prolonged period.

Rape Crisis centres fulfil an important function, and one that is hardly recognised by the state at national level. Because of the services provided to thousands of women every year, local authorities and charities are increasingly providing financial support, but the organisation is also important as an independent agency with experience of dealing with, and challenging, male violence. It has submitted evidence to a number of parliamentary select committees but is not among the organisations regularly consulted by the Home Office about victims' issues, presumably because of its critical political stance – which encourages service users and the public to consider and challenge the causes of sexual violence.

Women's Aid

Women's Aid refuges provide emergency accommodation and legal advice for women and children experiencing 'domestic' violence, but they do much more than this. They also support women recovering from violence, help them to obtain legal protection and representation, and assist them in dealing with other official agencies. Where court action is involved, they liaise with the courts on behalf of some women. Assistance is provided with finding appropriate housing when people are ready to move on and children living in refuges for long periods are helped with their educational and other needs. Some refuges are also able to provide outreach support, to help residents resettle after they leave. In some places advice surgeries are also provided in the community, particularly in rural areas. In addition to providing these direct services, most Women's Aid groups are represented on a local Domestic Violence Forum and involved in active liaison with local statutory agencies, including the police, probation, social and housing services. They also carry out staff training for these and other agencies, and fulfil a wider educational role through campaigning activities (Mullender 1996).

The refuge movement's first priority is to provide safe places for women and children to go to and, in a context of scarce resources, this may mean that educational and campaigning work has to be suspended at times (Mullender 1996). The ethos of the movement is one of self-help and mutual support, and residents obtain support from one another as well as from staff. The collective nature of the accommodation may be stifling for residents at times, but it does at least bring home to people that, 'If me, her and her have all been battered, it can't be all of us faults' (refuge resident quoted by Mullender 1996, p.267).

It is this collective approach which differentiates the feminist-inspired, women-only agencies from the mainstream victims' agencies, along with the emphasis upon survival as opposed to victimhood and the insistence on encouraging women to 'ask why'. Male violence is not taken as a given, women are enabled to examine its origins and the structures which support it and the collective nature of refuge accommodation facilitates group discussion of this kind by using an empowerment model (Mullender and Ward 1991). Refuge staff work with, rather than for, the residents, respecting and trying to enhance their self-determination (Lupton 1994).

In the UK refuges have always found it difficult to obtain adequate funding, no doubt partly because of the way in which they work and the resultant critical stance towards state agencies. In North America funding is more generous but the refuge movement there has had to adapt its non-hierarchical, campaigning style of working in exchange for adequate financial support from the state, moving towards a more traditional model of service provision (Lupton 1994).

Only a minority of UK refuges receive regular financial support from local authority departments and the provision and distribution of refuge places is patchy and illogical as a result (WAFE 1992). Where community care funding arrangements have been flexibly interpreted, local authorities have been able to provide secure funding for refuge workers' salaries (Mullender 1996) but, even then, the emphasis has been upon quantifiable outputs, which tends to detract attention from the refuge movement's wider aims and from its understanding of male violence as a social, rather than an individual or family, issue (Lupton 1994).

Given the increasing pressure upon social workers and other professionals to deal with their clients' problems individually rather than collectively, the continued existence of a collectively-run refuge movement is a tribute to its persistence and determination. There is a danger that Victim Support schemes, by moving into the area of work already covered by Women's Aid, may threaten the continued autonomous existence of the refuge movement, which remains chronically underfunded: 'The rise of VS and its expansion into the area of wife assault may be offering local and central government a cheaper and more politically acquiescent alternative to feminist-inspired women's groups' (Lupton 1994, p.72).

However, the victims' movement is becoming increasingly sophisticated politically and there are signs that such trends are being combated by careful inter-agency work at local level (see Chapter Six). Women's Aid has, for many years, operated under the umbrella of a national federation, which considerably strengthens the hand of local refuges when they are threatened by the actions of other agencies which also have a national structure with which the federation can engage and negotiate.

Support After Murder and Manslaughter

Support After Murder and Manslaughter (SAMM) is a self-help organisation formed by people bereaved as a result of murders to help others in the same position. Originally named 'Parents of Murdered Children', it subsequently broadened its remit to cover all murder and manslaughter cases. Its guiding principle is that it 'actively seeks the promotion of good health, both mental and physical, for those bereaved through homicide in order that they may learn to live positively with their tragedy in the future' (SAMM 1997).

It also seeks to improve public knowledge of the difficulties faced by those bereaved by homicide, to educate the relevant professionals and to campaign for improvements to the services and policies affecting its members.

Being small and specialised, it is in a position to take up the issues which particularly concern its members and to express their views strongly and authoritatively. Its national office is located in Victim Support's headquarters, which, perhaps, gives it access to a degree of influence it might not otherwise have. Its effectiveness is limited, however, because most of its work is done by individual volunteers in their spare time. While the fact that all its volunteers have lost relatives as a result of murders means that they are able to put its message across very powerfully, this can also be a disadvantage. Some SAMM volunteers have trained as counsellors but even they must find it difficult at times to stand back from the strong feelings expressed by other people trying to cope with the murder of a loved one. The organisation's credibility is diminished in some people's eyes by its self-help ethos and by its advocacy of harsher punishment for offenders (Williams 1996). From the point of view of survivors, however, SAMM volunteers understand their situation in a way nobody else can and the advice and support they can offer is invaluable. The campaigning role of the group is relatively low-key, but when it speaks on behalf of survivors of murder and manslaughter, its voice is uniquely authoritative. For example, its argument for probation work with survivors to be carried out by specialist staff (Nettleton, Walklate and Williams 1997) is hard to dismiss in view of its members' experience (see the section on the probation service later in this chapter).

There are, currently, thirteen SAMM groups and, apart from two paid staff at its national office, it is run entirely by volunteers. Its active membership consists of a little over a thousand people and its funding is from charitable sources and a grant from the Home Office, secured with the help of Victim Support national office (SAMM 1997).

Case study

The case study in Chapter Three (which described Albert and Mary's reactions to the murder of their daughter Susan) demonstrated some of the issues relating to SAMM. Its volunteers know from first-hand experience what survivors are likely to be going through and they can offer genuine, empathetic support. The volunteer may have found it therapeutic to put the experience of coping with a murder to use in helping others. While there is clearly a danger that volunteers may become over-involved (and their ability to help will then diminish), the existence of SAMM has undoubtedly increased the availability of well-informed help for survivors of murder victims. SAMM can also take up issues arising from individual cases, and wider concerns about the criminal justice system, because, as a small and specialist group, it has good communications with its volunteers and a sense of common purpose.

Other self-help organisations

SAMM has been used as an example of the smaller, self-help victim support agencies. In England and Wales there are others, such as Victims of Violence – which is local to one region (Merseyside) – and Mothers Against Murder and Aggression – which campaigned to prevent bookshops from stocking a revised biography of child murderer Mary Bell (Burrell 1998). In some areas the larger organisations are complemented by smaller groups, such as Women Against Rape – which provides advice, support and counselling for women who have suffered sexual violence as well as campaigning for changes in the law (HMIP 1998). Although they provide valuable services and an important platform for their members' grievances, no attempt is made here to describe all such groups – not least because some have proved quite short-lived and most are small, local and insecurely funded.

It is clear from the North American experience that such organisations can command considerable influence – sometimes, indeed, their political achievements seem quite out of proportion to their size. Mothers Against Drink Driving, for example, has brought about changes in the law in a number of American states.

In terms of potential assistance for victims and survivors, these organisations are remarkably effective in obtaining publicity and in reaching out to those who wish to contact them. This is due, in part, to the role of police officers and others in the statutory agencies who refer people to them, and partly, also, to their own publicity and fundraising efforts. While there is no doubt that they can prove to be a thorn in the side of the statutory agencies, they have an important role in publicising the lived experience of victims, as well as in providing direct personal support.

Statutory agencies

The police

As the first agency with which most victims of crime come into contact, as well as the most powerful and best resourced, the police clearly have a vital role in supporting victims of crime. It has been clear throughout this book that victims and survivors look to the police for advice, information and help but that they are not always completely satisfied with the service they receive. What role should be fulfilled by the police and how might the police response to victims be improved? Rather than try to answer these questions comprehensively, which would require a book in itself, this section describes the best practice adopted by a number of police forces. Issues of relations between the police and other agencies are considered further in a later section.

Victims, as potential witnesses, are important to the police when they are preparing cases for prosecution. Good witness care can improve the quality of witnesses' evidence and increase the chance of a successful prosecution. This line of reasoning has led some police forces, in recent years, to put increased resources into witness care. While this way of thinking might be criticised for its instrumental attitude to victims/witnesses, it appears that improved practices and attitudes towards witnesses may have positive spin-offs for victims in general. Similarly, many police initiatives aimed at protecting vulnerable witnesses, including those subject to intimidation, also produce more general improvements in services. In what follows the work of the Witness Care Department of Staffordshire Police is used to illustrate such developments, but it is only one of a number of British police forces which have recently improved their victim/witness care policies. Similar initiatives have also been taken in Canada, Japan and the USA (Mawby and Walklate 1994; Schulman 1997).

The assertion that witness care pays dividends in terms of improved relationships and better evidence in court is borne out in Merlyn Nuttall's account of her own case: 'The police gave the investigation 110 per cent. I felt that they were sensitive to me and kept very little from me. They therefore got the best from me, and vice versa' (Nuttall and Morrison 1997, p.127).

But the quest for evidence is not the only reason for taking care of victim/witnesses. They have needs which ought to be met and which they tend to expect the police to meet (Anderson and Leitch 1996; Hood 1998). This has been recognised in Staffordshire, where the Witness Care Department responds to victims' expressed needs as well as contacting all the victims of crime falling into certain categories regarded as vulnerable (such as child witnesses or victims, murder cases, racially-motivated offences and sexual offences) (Hood 1997). The support available ranges from an information leaflet to an escort to court and follow-up visits. In cases of serious intimidation physical police protection can be provided and offenders are prosecuted, but in lesser cases other forms of contact are used to encourage fearful witnesses to attend court when called. This fits in well with the demands made in the statement of victims' rights published by Victim Support (Victim Support 1995).

Merlyn Nuttall also praised the system of appointing a police liaison officer as a point of contact for the victims of serious offences: she wrote of her liaison officer: 'She had guts, determination and persistence, and she had an innate sense of right and wrong ... I trusted her completely ... She was one in a million' (Nuttall and Morrison 1997, p.66).

Such staff need institutional support, however. Nuttall goes on to record that the officer concerned suffered secondary victimisation, had nightmares about the attack she was investigating and became so involved that she felt compelled to work on the case in her own time. Lees (1997), in her otherwise extremely critical comments about police investigations of rape, pays tribute to the 'particularly impressive' work of such liaison officers.

Another aspect of rape investigations which raises concern is the use of male police surgeons (see above). Nuttall complains of being examined by an insensitive male doctor, and medical examinations were 'described by almost all the women as a horrific endurance test and several described it as utterly degrading' in Lees' research (1997, p.182). Although female victims requiring forensic examination should be given the choice of being seen by a woman doctor, this seems to be routinely ignored in practice (Temkin 1996). Some police services have responded to criticism by setting up rape and child abuse suites, away from police stations, where people can be interviewed, medically examined and offered support in a less threatening environment (Mawby and Walklate 1994). Such suites usually have predominantly female staff.

Police awareness of the vulnerability of particular types of victims is also increasing. Victim Support (1995) has called for witnesses vulnerable by reason of age or learning disabilities to be interviewed in the presence of an impartial person (a 'responsible adult' in the words of the Police and Criminal Evidence Act of 1984, which protects the rights of vulnerable suspects). The use of a third party to protect the rights of vulnerable witnesses is also recommended as good practice by Johns and Sedgewick (1999). Given the extent to which cases are currently failing to get to court where there are victims or witnesses with learning disabilities, police interests would seem to coincide with those of the witnesses themselves in such cases. One reason for such difficulties is that the counselling needed by vulnerable victims is frequently confused by police and prosecutors with 'coaching' them to say particular things in court, although counselling can certainly be provided in ways which avoid this pitfall (Bond 1998; Sanders et al. 1997). A different kind of vulnerability – to repeat victimisation and violent reactions to the reporting of offences – is recognised by the police in some areas where specialist units have been set up to respond to reports of domestic violence. This tendency was accelerated by the publication of a Home Office circular on the subject in 1990 (Mawby and Walklate 1994).

The police have an important role in ensuring that victims and witnesses are made aware of any bail conditions when the accused is allowed to go free pending trial. Judge Schulman's report on the deaths of Rhonda and Roy Lavoie in Manitoba, Canada, recommended that victims of male violence be routinely made aware of such changes in circumstances which, as that case graphically showed, could seriously affect the victim's safety. The report went on to say that there was a need for a system 'to ensure that victims receive immediate notification of all orders made in connection with outstanding charges against the offender and that they understand the meaning and significance of the orders. An information line, which the victim can call to learn whether the offender's application for judicial interim release was successful, should be initiated' (Schulman 1997, p.49). In the Lavoie case, and no doubt in others, such an arrangement could have saved lives. It has been incorporated in the Witness Care policy adopted by Staffordshire Police.

There are wider issues concerning the transmission of information between the police and victims of crime. Indeed, information is one of the needs most frequently identified in research about victims and communications failures are among the most frequent complaints of those victims expressing dissatisfaction with the service they receive from the courts and the police (Anderson and Leitch 1996; Mawby and Walklate 1994). Since 1988 the Home Office has been exhorting the police to improve their procedures for keeping victims informed, but progress has been patchy. A simple procedural change has led to considerable change in some areas: the form on which statements are taken by the police includes a tear-off information sheet about local services for victims and witnesses, including the name of the officer responsible for keeping the victim or witness informed (Hood 1997).

The Victim's Charter also requires the police to improve their arrangements for keeping victims informed, but here, too, implementation has been patchy (Mawby and Walklate 1994). Victim Support (1995) states that 'It is now general practice for police to give victims a contact telephone number, the name of the officer responsible, and progress reports' (p.20) but the research literature is less reassuring. Lees (1997), for example, reports that 'several women [in her study] commented on the poor flow of information on the progress of their case; many received no information whatsoever' (p.182).

Temkin (1997), while noting that most of the rape complainants she interviewed were positive about the treatment they received from the police, also noted that a significant minority were disappointed with 'lack of contact, lack of help and support and lack of information and advice [which in some cases] led victims to withdraw consent to prosecution' (p.517). There were cases in which police officers themselves felt that their contact with victims was inadequate, a failure they attributed to lack of time and pressure of work. This is particularly unfortunate if it results in prosecutions not reaching court: it is likely to reduce victims' confidence in the police and the whole criminal justice process. Again, the Staffordshire model attempts to deal with this problem by providing everyone who gives a statement with a contact number for the Witness Care Department, which will chase up any queries on their behalf as well as ensuring that 'vulnerable' victims are contacted in a more proactive way (Hood 1997).

Police inaction in the face of reported crime also arouses criticism from the public. Defining some offences (particularly sexual assaults and 'domestic' violence) as 'no-crime' and taking no further action may be justifiable in terms of resource constraints but it does nothing to increase public confidence in the criminal justice system. Given what we know about the likelihood of rape and sexual violence being committed by a man known to the woman, it is important that the police and prosecution service should change their culture of suspicion of such allegations (see Lees 1997; Mawby and Walklate 1994).

Mawby and Walklate (1994) note that police responses to offences such as burglary vary between countries – giving the example of France, where it is rare for police to visit the complainant's home. This is increasingly true in British cities, where a crime number may be given over the telephone for insurance purposes but little is thought likely to be gained by trying to collect evidence at the scene of the crime. Not surprisingly, members of the public in inner-city areas, whose only contact with the police is to report a break-in, feel aggrieved that they receive so little response. There is clearly an issue of police resources and priorities involved here, particularly at a time when rates of recorded crime are falling but violent crime continues to increase.

One response to public disquiet about the failure to take male violence seriously has been mandatory charging. This was discussed in Chapter Two in the context of 'zero tolerance' campaigns. In essence, it involves a pro-arrest policy on the part of the police combined with a specialist response by the prosecution service and the courts. This avoids falling into the trap of enshrining zero tolerance rhetoric in policy and practice without doing anything to protect complainants, and is discussed further as an example of inter-agency collaboration in the next section. Under the mandatory charging system, 'domestic' assaults are redefined as serious offences and there is agreement that 'rigorous prosecution should be pursued, but not at the expense of the victim' (Ursel 1998, p.77). In Winnipeg this strategy has met with high rates of public approval and the zero tolerance approach has avoided being co-opted as part of a law and order campaign, ensuring that the complainants are empowered rather than being manipulated for political reasons.

Policing priorities are subject to political debate and to consequent policy changes. General insensitivity to victims of crime may be more difficult to change. Mawby and Gill (1987) suggested that the police tended to underestimate the seriousness of the problems faced by victims and to pay most attention to the needs of those who were apparently vulnerable in terms of their old age and physical frailty, particularly if they lived alone. Since it is the attitudes of the front-line officers which are likely to make the first and most influential impression upon victims and witnesses of crime, it is they who most need to be trained to respond in an appropriately caring and constructive way. The police, to whom crime is routine, should, nevertheless, remain sensitive to its impact upon victims who experience it as individuals, and not only because of their age or physical health. Victims feel a need to be reassured, not least by the police, and to be recognised as someone with a legitimate grievance. This is not always recognised by police officers: 'Many victims express dissatisfaction with police officers who are distrustful, callous or cynical. Such observations are often viewed as evidence of secondary victimization' (Van Dijk 1985, cited by Mawby and Walklate 1994, p.97).

Mullender (1996) notes that changing government policies and wider social attitudes towards 'domestic' violence have gradually led to more constructive police attitudes to women reporting abuse. This has occurred partly as a result of the establishment of specialist units to deal with such violence, as with rape and child abuse. The Staffordshire model extends this further, making specialist contact available to all witnesses and victims of crime, and Her Majesty's Inspector of Constabulary has promoted it as an example of good practice which should be emulated by other areas (HMIC 1997).

Although the appointment of specialist staff is one way to improve police responses to victims, the question of operational staff attitudes towards victims remains important. The Witness Support model is likely to lead to some changes as it requires ordinary police officers to explain the service available to victims when they are taking statements. The specialist unit also has an educational and promotional role, both in terms of taking up any problems identified by individual victims and also by participating in staff training and inter-agency work. For example, the induction of new constables in Staffordshire now includes an exercise which requires them to find out what support services are available to victims of serious assaults, both from the police and in the wider community (Hood 1998).

Since the culture of hierarchical organisations is notoriously difficult to change, and such change has to be addressed on many different fronts simultaneously (Chan 1997), one of the keys to changing police attitudes to victims would seem likely to lie in staff training. Victim Support (1995) has strongly advocated changes in this area, arguing that police responses to victims should be informed by what is known about their likely needs and the potential damage caused by poor treatment at the hands of criminal justice personnel. The 1986 Home Office Circular referred specifically to the need to avoid interviewing rape complainants in such a way that they were made to feel under suspicion themselves, but police officers need to be trained to deal with all victims in ways which treat them with respect, avoid stereotyping them and show commitment to keeping them informed (Temkin 1997). While there is clearly much to be done, the police response to victims has been changing quite rapidly as a result of initiatives in the fields of training, central government and local policies, legal reforms – including the Victim's Charter, external pressures from the Inspector of Constabulary and women's groups among others – and local political pressures.

The prosecution service

In England and Wales the Crown Prosecution Service (CPS) is responsible for decisions about whether to take criminal cases to court, and for prosecuting them. Responsibilities for contact with witnesses and victims of crime are shared with the police. Since the publication of the first Victim's Charter in 1990, and the *National Standards for Witness Care* in 1996 (Trials Issues Group 1996), the CPS has had much greater responsibility for liaison with victims than in the past. (Local Trials Issues Groups have been set up to bring the CPS and other agencies together to improve arrangements for the care of witnesses and victims attending specific courts.)

Originally set up in 1987 as part of an attempt to prevent further miscarriages of justice arising from the previous system, under which the police themselves made decisions about whether to prosecute and then collated the evidence, the CPS has been dogged from the beginning by underfunding (Lees 1997). Many of its duties also overlap with those of the police and there has, until recently, been a lack of clarity as to where responsibility for keeping victims informed about cases should lie. As a result, the needs of victims have not always been well served. The CPS has found it difficult to supply the other criminal justice agencies with the information they need and has resisted attempts to require it to provide information directly to victims (Mawby and Walklate 1994). The consequence has been that, in many cases, victims are not kept informed about decisions and the police and probation services have insufficient information about victims' wishes and needs.

For example, the decision to drop a case because there is not enough evidence or because, for one reason or another, a prosecution is seen as unlikely to be in the public interest can cause distress and confusion to victims. Such decisions need to be explained, but until recently there has been no procedure to ensure that this is done. Fortunately, local Trials Issues Groups in most areas have now agreed procedures which should prevent communication failures of this kind in the future. Similarly, information should now routinely be passed on to other criminal justice agencies in such a way that courts can make appropriate decisions about compensation and about protecting vulnerable witnesses from undue distress while they give evidence, and probation officers should be enabled to provide the courts with information about the effects of crimes upon victims as part of their pre-sentence reports. Since all the necessary information is collected and collated by the CPS, the issue is mainly one of procedures and resources – but the prosecution service remains under-resourced, so considerable commitment will be needed before these improvements are consistently implemented.

Recent evidence suggests that difficulties persist. The issue of information is a crucial one. One of the fundamental concerns raised by victims everywhere is that the criminal justice system could do more to keep them informed. Yet those interviewed about their experience of magistrates' courts complained of being called to attend court only to be told when they got there that the case had been adjourned, not being given information about court procedures and not even being told what to do when they arrived at court (Plotnikoff and Woolfson 1998). These findings are very similar to those of previous research conducted seven years earlier (Raine and Smith 1991). Not only are such failures of communication distressing to individual victims, they also make people in general more reluctant to report crime for fear of having their time wasted (Saini et al. 1997).

Some concern has also been expressed about the ways in which the CPS makes decisions, but the responsibility here lies with its political masters rather than with the service itself. Prosecutors are bound by a code of conduct which restricts their discretion to a considerable extent, and one of the underlying principles is to avoid unnecessary expense in mounting cases which may subsequently collapse. Although the Victim's Charter requires the CPS to take account of victims' interests when deciding whether prosecutions are in the public interest (Home Office 1990), this is not usually done directly. Part of the reason is the laudable desire to avoid raising false hopes or making victims feel responsible for the decisions made (Victim Support 1995), but there is a lack of openness about the process which means that, inevitably, there are many cases where victims feel aggrieved about what is decided. Often, people are not even told that a case has been dropped, let alone why, despite the requirement to 'give appropriate weight to the views/wishes of the victim' (STIG 1997, p.10) and to make information available to the police so that decisions can be explained to victims (Home Office 1990).

Victims attending court are likely to want to be involved in the process in a variety of ways. In 1993 the Royal Commission on Criminal Justice recommended that prosecution barristers should introduce themselves to victims at court, but this is still not being done consistently. Perhaps of greater concern is the practice of plea-bargaining, whereby serious charges are dropped by the CPS in order to avoid the expense of a trial (Lees 1997; Mullender 1996), although, again, the overriding imperative is political or financial and outside the control of prosecutors.

The concept of the public interest is an ambiguous one and prosecutors have to devise rules of thumb in order to make sense of it in practice. It is arguable that some types of offenders are more likely to offend again and that they should, therefore, be prosecuted with particular vigour. Mullender (1996) makes this case, for example, in respect of men who commit serious offences of violence against female partners, plead guilty at a late stage to a relatively minor charge in order to avoid a trial, and go on to abuse other women. Lees (1997) makes a similar point in respect of marital rape and murders, with chilling case examples of offenders freed to attack the same woman again. In the end the public interest either has to be defined more explicitly or prosecutors will have to continue making the best of a bad job, deciding pragmatically on individual cases and trying to balance issues such as finance with public protection and victims' interests.

There are obvious problems with the current system, under which decisions are made on the basis of 'common sense' without all the relevant information. As noted in Chapter Two, this leads to discrimination against people with learning and communication difficulties who may be regarded by prosecutors as incapable of giving credible evidence. People who are at particular risk of victimisation, such as women with severe learning difficulties, are thus left vulnerable to further offences when properly trained professionals or groups such as WILD and People First could help them to make their case if they were involved at the appropriate time (Mullender 1996). Although the National Standards for Witness Care require special provisions to be made for all vulnerable witnesses (defined as people with mental and physical disabilities or mental illness, children, victims of sexual, domestic and racially-motivated crime and those experiencing or fearing intimidation), many professionals working in the courts are unaware of these arrangements. Not surprisingly, special arrangements are often not made (Plotnikoff and Woolfson 1998). There is also a strong case for adding a number of other groups to the list of vulnerable witnesses, including those whose first language is not English and other people with communication difficulties. While the inter-agency discussions mentioned above, and initiatives such as the specialist police unit described in the previous section, are likely to improve matters, change in this area is overdue. If the criminal justice system fails to treat victims and witnesses with respect, it undermines its own reputation and legitimacy.

As with the police, there is a need for more and better staff training in the area of victims' needs and rights. National Standards and policies are of no use if the staff involved do not know about them (Plotnikoff and Woolfson 1998) and do not understand the effects of victimisation upon the people they are making decisions about.

This discussion has concentrated upon the Crown Prosecution Service in England and Wales. There are similar arrangements in Scotland and the principle of separating prosecution from detection is accepted in most other legal systems. Prosecutors are charged with supporting and liaising with victims and witnesses in many countries, but the international research literature shows that the difficulties described in this section are by no means unique (see, for example, Joutsen 1987; Mawby and Walklate 1994; Wemmers 1996; Wemmers and Zeilstra 1991). In this respect, North American arrangements are more sophisticated than in most parts of Europe, having been first devised in the 1970s and refined over subsequent decades (Mawby and Walklate 1994; see also the Canadian case study later in this chapter).

Probation

In this section the process of introducing a new area of probation work in England and Wales – with victims of crime – will be used to illustrate some of the opportunities and problems involved in combining responsibilities for offender supervision and victim support.

Although probation officers in England and Wales have served on the committees of local Victim Support schemes, Women's Aid and Rape Crisis centres for many years, and have always worked with victims in an *ad hoc* way, they only acquired formal responsibility for work with victims in 1990 (Home Office 1990, 1996). Their main duties in this area are:

- providing courts with information about offenders, including their attitudes towards their victims, and providing information in the same pre-sentence reports about the impact of offences upon victims

- maintaining contact with victims of more serious offences after offenders are convicted in the higher (Crown) courts, in order to take the victims' wishes into account when decisions are eventually made about temporary release and the conditions under which prisoners may be released under supervision

- supervising such prisoners after their release and ensuring that they comply with any conditions imposed

- liaising with social services departments about arrangements for the supervision of people convicted of offences against children

- working with offenders to encourage victim empathy and prevent further offending.

Quite apart from the teething problems which accompanied the sudden introduction of these new responsibilities (Kosh and Williams 1995), the requirement to work in these ways with victims of crime has been something of a shock to probation staff traditionally concerned mainly with offenders. Indeed, there was widespread opposition within the service to the Victim's Charter, particularly when it became clear that no new resources would accompany the new duties (Williams 1996a). However, since 1996 all area probation services have begun to implement the charter, albeit at different rates and in varying ways. These variations have been described by some probation staff as unjust because the service received by victims differs from place to place and access to justice should be equal in all parts of the country (Nettleton, Walklate and Williams 1997). This situation arose partly because the government of the day chose not to introduce the new system by means of primary legislation but by incorporating it in the Victim's Charter and in

Home Office circulars and practice guidance whose legal status was unclear. This gave resource-starved probation services an opportunity to delay implementing the arrangements by questioning their legal basis (Williams 1997). No doubt such problems will be overcome now that a new government has reiterated its commitment to the probation role in working with victims, but these initial difficulties may have soured relationships between probation and the voluntary agencies in some areas.

Like the other statutory organisations described above, the probation service has had to go through a process of cultural change in order to accommodate work with victims and reconcile it with the supervision of offenders. Although such a change has to some extent been achieved, some observers have noted that certain old habits die hard.

One example was discussed in Chapter Three, namely the tendency of probation officers trained to confront and challenge offenders' attitudes to try and approach their work with victims in the same spirit. It has also been observed that probation officers sometimes ignore aspects of the anti-social attitudes and behaviour of offenders under their supervision. This can be interpreted as collusion, although it may be done with good intentions (as part of the process of gaining the offender's trust or in order to concentrate upon other issues which seem more pressing at the time).

Mullender (1996) gives the example of a male offender under supervision who demonstrates abusive attitudes or behaviour towards his female partner. If the offence for which he was put on probation is one of dishonesty or a motoring matter, there is a temptation to regard his personal relationships as irrelevant. What mandate does the probation service have, in such a case, to question the probationer's attitudes towards gender issues and his behaviour towards his partner? However, as Mullender points out, the failure to pick up this issue may place women in danger and be taken by the offender as tacit permission or even approval for his behaviour. Worse, in some cases the issue is avoided because the supervisor's attitudes towards women subjected to male violence are ambivalent: 'Some individual probation officers still overtly or covertly blame women for provoking, tolerating, asking for, enjoying or seeking abuse' (Mullender 1996, p.204).

It is a short step from such confusion to overt victim blaming (see Chapters One and Two). Part of the problem here is that probation officers' work is organised, to a large extent, on the basis of individual 'cases', making it difficult to see and work on the level of wider social forces. As Mullender goes on to point out, 'domestic abuse is strikingly widespread and abusers are not lone monsters whose offending occurs in a vacuum. Rather, the roots of abuse lie in the social construction of masculinity and the nature of male offending is often an extension of this' (p.204).

The tradition of working mainly one-to-one with offenders, usually hearing little or nothing of the victim's perspective, has created an organisational culture particularly conducive to the individualisation of social problems. Many staff have come to welcome the new victim orientation precisely because it gives them a more rounded picture of the situation concerning individual offenders and the role of the criminal justice system as a whole. In individual cases it brings issues of risk to life and reminds workers of the need to protect past and potential victims as part of the main function of the service, which is to protect society and help individual offenders by preventing reoffending. Sexual violence is a particularly pertinent example because offenders may seem plausible and biddable within the supervisory relationship but probation officers collude with their offending if they do not probe more deeply than this (see the case example in Mullender 1996, p.211).

Work with perpetrators and survivors of 'domestic' and sexual violence offers an opportunity to transcend this tendency towards individualisation, a process which had begun well before the publication of the Victim's Charter, building upon feminist ideas about male offending against women and children. Not only are there voluntary organisations willing to work in partnership with statutory criminal justice agencies on this issue (discussed earlier in this chapter and further below) but there are also established and successful models of group work with offenders (see Cowburn, Wilson and Loewenstein 1992; Knox 1996; Mullender 1996; Pithers 1993; Williams 1996). Probation staff have developed practice in these areas, engaging in debate with colleagues in the outside agencies about important issues such as the appropriateness of teaching offenders anger management and assertion techniques, and the effectiveness of trying to cultivate victim empathy among serious offenders (see HMIP 1998; Mann 1996; Pithers 1993; WMPSSOU 1996).[1] Despite the long tradition of individualistic work, there

---

[1]   There is some disagreement about the benefits of working to engage offenders' empathy for their victims. There is evidence that empathy strengthens well-motivated offenders' resolve not to offend again and that those who understand the harm they have done to victims try harder to learn and practise relapse prevention skills. Empathy interferes with sexual arousal to rape in most offenders but it appears that the most aggressive rapists are not affected in this way. It can also be counter-productive to attempt to engage empathy too soon (HMIP 1998).

are signs that this is being transcended and that increased involvement with victims and their representative organisations since 1990 has improved probation officers' understanding of the social and structural origins of crime (NAPO 1997). Where group work is not practicable, report writing for the courts and supervision of convicted offenders have also been becoming more creative in the light of improved knowledge and training on work with high-risk clients (HMIP 1998).

The main rationale for probation work with victims of crime, apart from the lack of another suitable statutory agency equipped to carry it out, is the service's expertise in crime prevention. Here, too, there are signs that work with victims has helped to change the culture of the service. It was not unusual, in the early 1980s, for the surviving relatives of murder victims to move away from their home area when they heard that the offender was being considered for release. Now that victims are required to be consulted by probation officers prior to the completion of parole reports, it is much more common for the prisoner to move to a different part of the country on release, with supervising officers making arrangements which respect the known wishes of victims. It is now quite normal for life-sentence prisoners' release plans to be altered in response to information obtained from survivors in the course of such enquiries, a state of affairs which would have been unusual only five years ago in most parts of the country because probation officers simply did not have access to the necessary information.

More regular contact with victim support agencies and individual victims has probably also increased probation staff awareness of ways of protecting people from potential reoffending by known perpetrators of violence. Mullender (1996) gives the example of probation officers' potential role in advising and supporting abused women and referring them to specialist agencies such as Women's Aid. Although this is by no means new, it is likely to be happening more often now than in the past. Similarly, offenders motivated by racism or homophobia are now receiving closer attention from supervising probation officers (NAPO 1997).

It is now possible for enquiries conducted before prisoners are released to be carried out with the assistance of victim support agencies. Where a victim or survivor is known to such an agency, joint visits can be made by probation and Victim Support or Rape Crisis staff in order to reassure those being interviewed and build up the necessary trust (NAPO 1997).

The probation officer's greater involvement in advising on the decision on whether to release prisoners under the new arrangements should also serve to protect former partners from pressure to take violent men back into their homes. Whereas, in the past, probation officers were merely asked to prepare 'home circumstances reports' (sometimes written without interviewing the prisoner, let alone his or her victim/s), prisoners serving long sentences are no longer released without up-to-date information about victims being compiled by probation officers and submitted to the prison. In such circumstances probation officers are far less likely to succumb to pressure to accede to any plausible release plan: they have to go into some detail about risk factors and assure themselves that the plan is viable. In many cases the enquiries made of victims are now conducted by specialist staff who do not know the prisoner, making it easier for honest opinions to be expressed and harder for the prisoner's probation officer to miss cues (NAPO 1997). In evidence to HM Inspectorate of Probation, Women Against Rape argued that probation staff must avoid putting pressure upon the partners of violent offenders to accept them back into their homes (HMIP 1998) and this approach now commands general support.

These enquiries have, at times, been carried out insensitively (Kosh and Williams 1995; Nettleton, Walklate and Williams 1997), particularly in the early days when retrospective reports were being made about offences committed decades previously. Some probation services continue, due to resource constraints, to instruct their staff to obtain information from victims/survivors without offering any emotional support (see Nettleton, Walklate and Williams 1997). Indeed, there are those in Victim Support schemes who feel that their volunteers would be better equipped than busy probation staff to carry out this work: 'I think it would rather come from us rather than some poor person who is run off their feet with paperwork and hasn't got time to think' (co-ordinator quoted by Kosh and Williams 1995, p.17).

There was a reluctance on the part of some probation staff to entrust sensitive work to voluntary agencies, which may stem from a variety of concerns – for example, about confidentiality, the reliability of volunteers or the perception that such organisations and some of their volunteers have an anti-offender stance (Kosh and Williams 1995). There was also a rather patronising fear on the part of some probation staff that voluntary agencies might do more harm than good in such a sensitive area of work (Williams 1996a). Possibly, some workers also feared for their own jobs at a time when probation was facing large-scale redundancies and cuts in services.

However, there are signs that creative partnerships are being formed between probation services and voluntary organisations to deliver this service effectively, ensuring that appropriate support is available to anyone distressed by the interviews, and that it is now being carried out with considerable professionalism (HMIP 1998; NAPO 1997; Nettleton, Walklate and Williams 1997).

Regrettably, the probation service has tended to follow central government in limiting most of its contact with the voluntary sector to a single organisation, Victim Support, and, in most areas, the opportunity has not been taken to form partnerships with other groups. In a small number of areas, however, there are good links with such organisations (HMIP 1998; Nettleton, Walklate and Williams 1997). This is important because the service has funding powers which can help to maintain a vibrant and varied voluntary victim support sector. While such relationships may not always be easy (ACOP 1992), such inter-agency work is crucial in terms of its potential benefits for service users. If statutory services favour the 'official' voluntary agencies at the expense of groups which have been marginalised by central government (see Chapter Four), they are reproducing political discrimination against those expressing minority views and, in some cases, effectively barring potential service users from access to these groups and the services they provide. Since 1997, however, the Association of Chief Officers of Probation has begun to engage in dialogue with representatives of Rape Crisis and Women's Aid at national level and, in some areas, probation staff meet regularly with a range of victim support agencies – for example, through mutual involvement in a Domestic Violence Forum or Racial Harassment Forum.

One barrier to effective liaison between probation services and the voluntary sector has been the funding mechanism governing probation service partnerships with outside organisations. A number of Victim Support schemes told Nettleton, Walklate and Williams (1997) that they would prefer a more flexible arrangement than the contractual model favoured by the Home Office, and Hague (1997) reported similar findings. The tendency to characterise victims of crime as 'consumers' of criminal justice stems from the same mindset among central government civil servants, and the problems this has caused were discussed at some length in Chapter Four.

The need for cultural change has been a recurrent theme in this discussion of victim perspectives in statutory agencies. In probation, as in the police service, part of the solution to the problem of accommodating victims' concerns is the introduction of dedicated units and specialist staff charged with carrying out work involving victim contact. This allows for proper staff training and avoids conflicts of loyalties between the service's sometimes conflicting responsibilities towards offenders and victims (NAPO 1997). The examples of best practice identified by Nettleton, Walklate and Williams (1997) were in such specialist units, and such specialisation seems likely to offer the most constructive way forward.

As with the police and prosecution services, this discussion of probation work with victims has identified a number of staff training issues. Probation officers need to be trained to avoid the kind of collusion which has sometimes characterised their work with offenders, so that opportunities to protect actual or potential victims of crime arising in the course of offender supervision are not missed. Inter-agency training, ideally bringing together staff from voluntary and statutory agencies and volunteers working with victims, developed in partnership between the various groups, is likely to prove constructive (Mullender 1996). Probation officers need better initial training, paying attention to the subtleties of human interaction and the social causes of crime. Their 'victim awareness' should be developed at this early stage if they come to the training without experience of working directly with victims of crime, and all staff should receive such sensitisation (NAPO 1997; Williams 1999).

Other agencies

Space does not permit detailed consideration of the role of other agencies in work with victims and survivors but, in this section, a few of the relevant issues will be briefly touched upon.

There are clear implications in the discussion of the prosecution service (above) for those involved in the administration of courts and in day-to-day contact with victims. As court buildings are adapted or replaced, consideration is now being given to the need to avoid bringing victims and offenders face to face while they await court hearings. Courts are adapting their administrative procedures to avoid witnesses being called to court unnecessarily, to ensure that they are kept informed while they are waiting to give evidence and to share information about vulnerable witnesses with the other criminal justice agencies and take steps to provide video links or screens where appropriate.

Defence lawyers have a role in ensuring that victims and witnesses with communication or learning difficulties or other special needs are enabled to give evidence effectively and that witnesses who are in fear are reassured and their concerns communicated to the police and the courts. Where necessary, they should inform the trial judge of victims' special needs. The involvement of court officials and lawyers in local Trials Issues Groups has helped to raise their awareness of victims' needs and to improve practice in courts, although the process is likely to be long and slow.

The ramifications of victim awareness, in its broadest sense, are enormous and have an impact well outside the criminal justice system. Employers whose staff are attacked have, in many cases, long acknowledged their responsibilities towards them – for example, in arranging counselling and compassionate leave. Research in the Netherlands suggests that employees handling money can be prepared during staff training sessions for the possibility of being involved in a robbery, and that this preparation, which includes role-play and discussion of appropriate reactions to hold-ups, helps to avoid unduly adverse responses to victimisation when it does occur (Markus 1997). Increased awareness of issues affecting victims is likely to impinge on many unexpected areas.

References have been made on several occasions in previous chapters to the possibility that victims suffering adverse reactions might need professional help. In some cases this might be provided with the help of employers (as in the case of staff robbed in the course of their work) or through private medical insurance. Where it necessitates referral to the National Health Service, however, there are likely to be problems: there may be a long waiting list for an appointment and generalist psychiatrists may have little specialist knowledge of the needs of victims. Before referral to mental health services, enquiries need to be made about what kinds of help are available locally.

Inter-agency approaches to supporting victims

The different agencies involved in working with victims have a good deal to gain from working together and sharing their experience. While inter-agency collaboration is not a panacea (and some of the pitfalls are considered in Chapter Six), this is hardly surprising: 'To see any single policy or program as the solution is naive ... We must give up any search for single solutions and/or single institutions to blame' (Ursel 1998, p.80).

A number of initiatives have demonstrated the ways in which inter-agency work can sensitise criminal justice workers to the needs of victims of crime and provide opportunities for them to collaborate in meeting these needs. For example, the Home Office suggestion that police forces should become involved in every Domestic Violence Forum in their locality accelerated the establishment of a network of specialist police Domestic Violence Units and helped, over a period of time, to improve police responses to women reporting abuse. In such a local forum institutional barriers to change can be identified, discussed and surmounted or circumvented. Part of the problem previously was that no single agency had been responsible for the issue: an inter-agency forum can create a focus for taking ownership of the issues and finding ways of turning organisations previously seen as part of the problem into part of the solution (Mawby and Walklate 1994; Mullender 1996).

Apart from bringing the relevant agencies together to share their concerns, inter-agency work with victims can help to re-orientate the police, usually the most powerful of the organisations involved, towards a service role. Discussion with the other agencies helps to convince the police that the assistance they provide to members of the public is important in its own right, as well as helping catch criminals and having a legitimating function (Mawby and Walklate 1994).

A recognition by all the official agencies that they are there to serve the public, and that victims have entitlements and are making claims for additional rights, can ultimately lead to the empowerment of victims and their organisations. The Family Violence Courts in Winnipeg, Canada, offer an interesting case study in such potential benefits for victims of crime arising from successful partnerships between criminal justice agencies.

Case study

In the early 1980s the Attorney-General of Manitoba ordered that there should be a presumption in favour of pressing charges against perpetrators of spouse assault wherever there was a reasonable case. This reversed previous practice: the police had tended to avoid prosecuting in 'domestic' cases. The policy was popular with the public, with 85 per cent of respondents to an opinion poll in 1984 saying they supported it (Ursel 1998). In response the provincial government set up a new office to develop and fund wife-abuse services, giving a substantial fillip to the voluntary sector. In 1990 the Family Violence Court was set up in Winnipeg, taking over responsibility for all child, spouse and elder abuse cases. Its staff included specialist prosecutors as well as witness support workers and women's rights workers. Its remit was to deal with the increasing number of family violence cases more quickly, sensitively and appropriately than the existing, generic courts were able to (Ursel 1994).

Within a short period, the number of cases coming to court increased, charging and sentencing patterns changed substantially and public approval of the programme was sustained. The police increasingly charged men with offences of violence against their partners, and men and women who offended against children or older people in their care. The court sentenced more and more offenders to supervised treatment. In 1993 the police introduced a zero tolerance policy, removing all discretion in such cases and leaving the prosecution to decide which reported cases to take to court. This resulted in further increases in the number of people arrested and substantial press and public support: by 1995 the zero tolerance policy was supported by 80 per cent of respondents (87% of women and 71% of men) (Ursel 1998, p.76).

The number of offenders being put on probation increased considerably and the rate of use of other disposals changed significantly. Conditional discharges were used less often and suspended and immediate imprisonment more frequently than prior to the establishment of the specialist court (Ursel 1994). This was seen as a successful outcome in that the seriousness of 'domestic' violence was being acknowledged, but in the great majority of cases a treatment outcome meant that there was some optimism being expressed about the offender's potential to change.

One consequence was a rapid increase in the number of people sentenced to probation or prison with a requirement that they receive appropriate treatment. In 1992 the provincial Corrections Department created a specialist unit whose staff work with convicted family violence offenders and groups for abusers became much more readily accessible.

Although, in some respects, an example of the imposition of a policy (albeit a popular one) from the top-down, this case study also illustrates the potential for inter-agency collaboration in providing services to victims of crime. The Family Violence Court created a partnership between prosecution lawyers, witness support staff and women's rights workers (the latter groups both traditionally employed in voluntary agencies). It built upon a thriving culture of voluntary sector campaigning for effective sentencing for offenders and quality services for survivors. With changes in sentencing patterns, the corrections service responded to the need for groupwork activities which would challenge offenders' attitudes towards women, children and older people effectively.

Thus the statutory agencies were sensitised to victims' needs and concerns. The importance of implementing courts' sentences effectively is central to the efficient operation of probation and prisons, and changes in sentencing pattern were thus rapidly reflected in the nature of service provision: thus the corrections agency 'by virtue of some administrative restructuring, found its own legitimacy dependent upon the realisation of the very reforms advocated by women's groups, that is, the expansion of treatment groups for offenders' (Ursel 1997, p.266).

Similarly, the police had previously made changes to staff training, response rates to calls about 'domestic' violence and the procedures for protecting victims and witnesses and providing them with the information they need. Further changes are in hand as the result of an official enquiry into a murder case where these procedures were not followed as thoroughly as they should have been. In particular, the process of referring injured parties to women's advocacy programmes needs tightening up, as do police practices in relation to keeping records of complaints of abuse for future reference and action. Police procedures and practices are in future to be reviewed annually by an independent outside agency (Schulman 1997). Winnipeg police have certainly become more accustomed to the idea that they have responsibility for providing a high-quality service to victims of crime: they have a specialist unit which employs social work-trained staff to support and liaise with all victims of serious crime and provide information to the courts. Routine police training now includes the spousal assault policy and emergency response procedures, and beat police officers have been heavily involved in changing the police response to 'domestics' by no longer avoiding the issue but implementing the zero tolerance policy and arresting and charging suspects.

Prior to the establishment of the Family Violence Court, women who failed to appear as witnesses in cases of spousal abuse were, on occasions, charged with contempt of court and, sometimes, even imprisoned. This has not happened since 1990 and, indeed, a new legal strategy of 'testimony bargaining' has evolved. Prosecutors ask reluctant witnesses what outcome they would ideally like court cases to have and charges and recommended sentences are tailored accordingly. Faced with the prospect of a reduced charge and the likelihood of a community sentence, the perpetrator tends to plead guilty. 'This is not orthodox criminal justice procedure, but we know that orthodox procedure has often victimised the witness in domestic violence cases' (Ursel 1997, p.272).

Some time ago, Ursel (1997) recommended the establishment of specialist police units to respond to 'domestic' violence, and this is echoed in the report of the official enquiry (Schulman 1997). Such units would guarantee a sympathetic and well-informed response, at least to high-risk cases. But the process described in the case study has already done a good deal to empower people reporting family violence, largely as a result of effective collaboration between the various voluntary and statutory agencies involved.

This chapter has considered the respective roles of the various statutory and voluntary agencies involved in supporting victims and has begun to look at inter-agency partnership in improving such services. The concluding chapter continues the consideration of issues of partnership and suggests some changes to the current arrangements.

CHAPTER SIX

The Way Forward

This final chapter discusses the future of support for victims of crime. How can we give victims genuine choices? How can services, and liaison between them, be enhanced? The implications of the individual and agency case studies in earlier chapters for future policy are addressed with a view to suggesting positive policy changes for the future. The question of victims' rights is also revisited: are victims of crime a new social movement and, if so, how does this strengthen their position?

Inter-agency work: opportunities and problems

Where the statutory agencies are represented by staff sufficiently senior to command financial and other types of resources (Hague, Malos and Dear 1996; Smith, Paylor and Mitchell 1993), and where practitioners' concerns are also fully represented (including workers from the voluntary sector agencies), a co-ordinating group such as an inter-agency Domestic Violence Forum can help to improve service provision. Given that many would-be service users approach more than one agency, anything which improves co-ordination between agencies is likely to make services more accessible (Mullender 1996). Agency staff and volunteers gain access to better and more varied training opportunities through inter-agency work, networking is facilitated and agencies' policies are developed with an awareness of the context in which other organisations in the field operate. Effective and co-ordinated educational and campaigning work can take place, new projects can be initiated and good practice can be publicised and spread. Where necessary, recalcitrant agencies can be influenced to change their practices and special provision for minority groups which services would otherwise fail to reach can be initiated. In some areas arrangements have been made for abused women and children to join an inter-agency forum and advise it from a service user's perspective (Hague, Malos and Dear 1996).

Other models of inter-agency work are initiated by statutory organisations in order to meet their own objectives. These include the contracting out of specific areas of work and grant aid to other agencies. Under contracting arrangements, agreement is reached on the objectives of the partnership and the provider organisation is paid for its work according to that contract. Grant aid is more flexible: the statutory organisation identifies a community group whose aims are compatible with its own and provides financial assistance to it. When money changes hands in either of these ways, the relationship between the recipient and the purchaser is almost bound to change and co-ordinating activities of the kind discussed above can be distorted and disrupted by financial considerations. For example, a voluntary organisation which exists by fund-raising in its own community may change direction radically in response to the wishes of a local probation or social services department once the relationship between the two becomes a financial one. Smaller voluntary groups may lose their sense of purpose in the face of rapidly changing priorities. Many victim support agencies deliberately steer clear of such grant aid in order to protect their autonomy (Kosh and Williams 1995). Grant aid can, however, help local groups to achieve their own objectives where these are compatible with those of local statutory authorities. Some Rape Crisis centres and Women's Aid groups, for example, receive support, in money or in kind, from social services departments (see Chapter Five). In some areas probation services have made grants to the general funds of Victim Support schemes and, elsewhere, joint projects have been set up sharing the resources available to both organisations (Nettleton, Walklate and Williams 1997).

Experience has shown that a number of factors influence the success of inter-agency work between statutory agencies and groups supporting victims. No single agency should be allowed to dominate and the objectives of collaboration should be clear from the outset. Each partner agency needs to 'own' the work more or less equally and to allocate appropriate resources to it (in staff time, cash or kind). Information must be shared and progress monitored. Mechanisms for addressing cultural and other differences between agencies and their ways of working should be put in place. The distinctive approaches adopted by some victim support groups need to be understood and accepted by the other organisations, rather than subverted by a process of co-option. These lessons have been learnt from hard experience and it is much easier to set them out here than to put them into practice (see Kosh and Williams 1995; Mullender 1996; Sarkis and Webster 1995; Smith, Paylor and Mitchell 1993; for more detail).

As this might suggest, inter-agency work, both in the sphere of the Domestic Violence Forum and in other areas of victim support work, has been beset with difficulties in practice. The necessary conditions have often not been in place and attempts at partnership have, at times, created venues for conflict. More often, however, such conflict is avoided and, as a consequence, collaborative committees become mere talking shops or venues for moaning about the difficulty of achieving real change (Mullender 1996). Worse, they can become 'a smokescreen to disguise inaction' (Hague 1997, p.93), a public relations exercise without practical substance – sometimes even diverting resources away from direct service agencies or creating new demands on such groups through their publicity campaigns without generating any extra funding with which to carry out the work. Some come to be dominated by the most powerful agencies involved and achieve little – or if they are controlled by the police, they lose the trust of smaller groups or come to be seen as part of a strategy of widening social control through gaining information from community organisations (Walklate 1989).

It would seem that inter-agency work is most likely to succeed if it starts with achievable, practical tasks. Once the various organisations find successful ways of working together, these can be built upon. Inter-agency partnership should not be seen as an end in itself (as it so often seems to be in central government advice to local authorities) but should proceed from a desire to solve mutual problems. The probation service's increasingly constructive relationships with local Victim Support schemes in working with victims and survivors of offenders serving long prison sentences are an example, although the partnership was a difficult one in its early stages in many areas (see Chapter Four). Such collaboration between statutory and voluntary agencies can help to break down stereotypical views among staff and volunteers on both sides and also has the potential to improve understanding of the social factors underlying victimisation. Another example of improved inter-agency relationships resulting from collaborative work is the Family Violence Court, described in the case study in Chapter Five.

Victims and offenders

Criminal victimisation is often discussed without any consideration of the offenders responsible for it, except for a generalised expression of disapproval of their callousness. In some circumstances greater understanding of the motivation and background of offenders can be helpful to victims, as in the case of burglary victims who are reassured after finding out that their house was not deliberately targeted but was burgled by an opportunist offender who is unlikely to return (see Williams 1996). In many cases information about the offender can be helpful to victims in coming to terms with an offence and putting it behind them, and this is presumably the thinking behind the Victim's Charter's arrangements for the probation service to give victims of serious crime information about the release plans for the prisoners involved, discussed in Chapters Four and Five.

The attempt to treat victims and offenders as two completely separate groups is, in some ways, understandable but it is also very misleading. Not only have many offenders previously suffered criminal victimisation but a significant proportion of victims are themselves ex-offenders (see Chapter Two). In the case of childhood sexual abuse there is probably a link between the consequences of such victimisation (which may include low self-esteem, reduced educational achievement, depression and, in some cases, post-traumatic stress) and the disproportionate number of young and adult offenders reporting having experienced such abuse (NAPO 1997; Peelo et al. 1992; Widom 1991).

The artificial separation of victims from offenders results partly from the ideal type of a victim – the notions that victims of crime are usually vulnerable, engaged in respectable activities in a reputable place at the time of the offence, have no personal relationship with the offender and suffer physical harm at the hands of someone stronger than them (Christie 1986; Hartless et al. 1995). 'Real' victims are also commonly conceptualised as having been co-operative with the police and having done nothing to provoke the offence, and it helps if they are members of the majority racial community (Strobl 1997). It is clear from the case studies and from the literature reviewed throughout this book that the idealised notion of a victim of crime is often not borne out by the facts – and that each aspect of the ideal illustrates a conflict between 'common sense' ideas about victims of crime and the reality. Such idealisations often have an underlying social and political function, and it is important to see beneath them.

Victims of crime are not, in fact, always pleasant or blameless people. They need not belong to vulnerable groups (although in many cases they do) and the offender need not be stronger than them. They often fail to report offences to the police or conceal important aspects of the story. Many are partly to blame for what happened to them, as in the case of most drunken assaults – where both the perpetrator and the injured party tend to have over-indulged. A large proportion of offenders are known to their victims, often in intimate relationships. Why might these facts fail to fit the 'ideal' victim?

One obvious reason is that the agencies seeking help in tracking down offenders and in supporting victims are reluctant to introduce such ambiguities into the discussion. The police officer appealing for witnesses, the solicitor arguing that a victim should receive compensation or the street collector asking for money for a victim support agency cannot afford to get into this level of debate: it would undermine what they are trying to do. This is all the more true for politicians seeking to parade their credentials as supporters of law and order and campaigners for victims' rights. There is no room for moral ambiguity or intellectual complexity when public support needs to be enlisted.

Another motive for maintaining a rigid distinction between victims and offenders is that victims have an understandable psychological need to be reassured that they were not to blame for what happened – a need which should definitely be met, in most cases, in order to assist them with the process of recovering from victimisation (see the discussion of victim blaming in Chapter One and the arguments for reassuring victims that they are not to blame in Chapter Two). This need can, however, be distinguished from the failure to recognise, when making policy, that there are, in fact, categories of victims who could be better protected if their own role in the process were better understood and that victims' own prior experiences may make them more vulnerable to further offences. Of course, the primary blame for crime rests with offenders but, as Walklate (1989) points out, what she calls 'offender blaming strategies' which pretend that the best solution to crime is to penalise offenders more harshly have very limited effectiveness when it comes to reducing victimisation rates. To concentrate upon individual offenders neglects the structural causes of crime. To pretend that imprisoning more offenders helps victims is simply misleading.

This structural issue is, perhaps, the most important reason for maintaining a rigid distinction between victims and offenders: once this differentiation is blurred, questions about the social factors underlying crime are raised. The maintenance of an artificial divide keeps the discussion safely on the individual level, whereas any acknowledgement of the commonalities between many victims and offenders raises awkward questions of the kind discussed in Chapter Two. Both victims and convicted offenders are over-represented among the young, the poor and the oppressed. Raising such issues undermines the individualisation process which criminal justice agencies and staff employ to distance themselves from such social issues. This is discussed further in the next section.

Victims of crime – a social movement?

The growth of agencies of and for victims of crime was described in Chapter One and it is clear that the support of victims is increasingly recognised in many societies as a matter of concern which merits financial and other kinds of support. Throughout this book references have been made to specialist staff working in statutory and voluntary agencies to provide services to victims, and also to initiatives taken to improve their position. Does this activity constitute a social movement and what difference does the answer make to victims themselves?

The process of recognising the needs of crime victims began, in many countries, with the introduction of state-provided financial compensation. This was a response to a specific demand voiced by individuals and by nascent victims' organisations. In some places, once this demand was met, victims made no further concerted demands and the issue died down again, at least for a time. In England and Wales, for example, once a compensation scheme was established in 1964, 'the interest which had been aroused in victims of crime dissipated' (Mawby and Walklate 1994, p.76). This is a common characteristic of single-issue campaigns: once their central demand is met, they go quiet. Scott (1990) gives the example of the suffragettes' demand for votes for women. However, such a campaign raises the awareness of those involved in it and, when new issues arise, it can rapidly re-form, as did the suffrage campaign.

About the time when interest in victims of crime was dying down in the UK, the issue re-emerged in the USA. Crime had become a federal election campaigning point and the black civil rights and feminist movements were simultaneously undergoing a revival (Mawby and Walklate 1994). These movements both demanded measures to improve the position of survivors of hate crimes and populist political campaigns on crime included calls for victims' needs to be met. These demands coincided and the disparate organisations calling for similar types of change represented a powerful, if accidental, combination. These issues came to the fore somewhat later in the UK with the establishment, in the early 1970s, of women-only organisations focusing on violence towards women and the later emergence of a mass anti-racist movement. By the mid-1970s the seeds of a national organisation for victims of crime were evident on both sides of the Atlantic with the formation of Victim Support in England and of NOVA in America.

Such activity is not in itself evidence that a new social movement was emerging. A social movement arises when members of excluded groups mobilise (or threaten to do so) to seek recognition and influence, and to demand changes affecting their interests. They are brought together by a sense of common identity, often augmented by discontent with the failure of the powers that be to recognise their case: 'When political parties become weak at representing particular interests, social movements can take their place and combine various groups – conservative, liberal or radical – into coalitions' (Weed 1995, p.1).

A process of 'domain expansion' is frequently pursued, whereby issues are brought to public awareness and claims are made about the need to tackle them and the best ways in which to do so (Best 1990; Scott 1990). As part of this process, new agencies assert their expertise and their fitness to address the issues themselves by providing services.

While domain expansion activity is a recognisable characteristic of Victim Support in the UK (see Chapter Five) and of other groups campaigning for victims' rights, which have consistently argued and demonstrated the need for new services for victims, it is questionable to what extent most crime victims identify with the description of themselves as victims – for many, it is a brief and transitory experience. Survivors of rape and murder may come together in campaigning organisations to demand changes to the law and politically-conscious members of oppressed groups may set up projects to support victims of hate crimes like racial and homophobic abuse (Jenness 1995), but victims of burglary are unlikely to feel the necessary group solidarity or sense of common identity to band together in this way.

A social movement can, however, accommodate temporary adherents and people whose commitment is limited to finding ways of meeting their own immediate needs. Indeed, it can gain increased legitimacy by incorporating such individuals and groups into its programme of demands and, as it gains access to those in power, it can, in turn, be incorporated by the state (Kirby 1995).

By providing services to victims in need, organisations making demands upon the state increase their own visibility. There is a sense in which the expansion of such services interacts with the domain expansion process: the demand for the service proves the existence and seriousness of the social problem it was set up to deal with. Thus victim assistance organisations set up by the American gay and lesbian movement over the last decade began by simply documenting abuse and assaults. This increased the reporting of such incidents under the Hate Crimes legislation and helped to make the case for providing funding to run advice and counselling services: 'visibility is a central resource for social movements and a central component for the successful construction of a social problem' (Jenness 1995, p.157).

This is not to suggest that there was no problem in the first place but rather to draw attention to the dynamics of the way in which the case for victims' needs to be met is socially constructed. Not only does the existence of hate crime increase people's sense of intra-group solidarity by demonstrating links between the personal and the political but the establishment of victim assistance programmes also provides an outlet for such feelings by giving people the chance to become volunteer counsellors. When victim assistance is combined with public education activities and training programmes for criminal justice professionals, a powerful mix of visibility and legitimacy can be achieved. Demands for state funding to support service provision and further educational activities then become all but irresistible.

While the prior existence of a potent, conspicuous and politically conscious social group such as the women's, black or lesbian and gay movement may accelerate change, the domain expansion process can help to create a movement around less well-focused issues such as criminal victimisation in general: 'in so far as all social movements are concerned to effect social change they are bound to... politicize areas of activity previously thought of as personal' (Scott 1990, p.143).

At a time of constraints upon public expenditure, any claim for resources is subjected to close scrutiny and is made in competition with many others. Claims for new rights and services are controversial and contested. The existence of organisations of and for victims provides a focus for the process of staking such claims, although there is a continuum of agencies ranging from the bureaucratised and professionalised Victim Support to smaller and more amateurish groups. Similarly, there is a range of social movements 'stretching from informal network-like associations to formal party-like associations' (Scott 1990, p.132).

At the informal end of the continuum, groups such as Women's Aid value a 'sense of autonomy in terms of organization and tactics of struggle' (Kirby 1995, p.71) and they may wish to protect their status as organisations *of* rather than *for* victims on the grounds that survivors bring a unique understanding of the nature of victimisation. In doing so they elevate personal experience to a political level and reject the individualising tendencies of the more 'official' victims' organisations.

Victim Support, on the other hand, gives up a degree of its autonomy by accepting central government funding and organising itself to meet Home Office priorities such as maximising the number of one-off visits to individual victims in their homes (see Chapter Five). It also – because of the way it is organised and financed and because of its history – tends to individualise issues around criminal victimisation. If (as recent crime prevention campaigns have suggested) anyone can become a victim of crime, victims' rights can come to be seen as essentially individualistic in nature (Elias 1990; Mawby and Walklate 1994). Only when criminal victimisation is explicitly linked to its higher incidence among members of oppressed groups and its social causes does it come to be seen as a social and political issue – an approach which Victim Support has generally avoided (see Chapters Four and Five). When victims of crime are portrayed as no more than consumers of criminal justice services, on the other hand, the 'official' victims' movement can be pacified with initiatives such as the Victim's Charter, which fail to respond to or even acknowledge the more radical demands of the wider victims' movement or to recognise the existence of excluded groups which are trying to claim rights (see Oliver 1996).

It would appear that there is indeed a victims' movement, at least in the 'developed' world, but that it is a varied and somewhat divided one. It may not meet the strict sociological criteria for a 'new' social movement because some of its adherents have only their victimisation in common and have no sense of solidarity with each other, but it is already a powerful force and it has the potential to become much more so. The concept of new social movements has, in any case, been challenged for over-emphasising the novelty of the involvement of social movements in the political process (Scott 1990): many identifiable social movements do not have all the characteristics of such a 'new' movement (for example, the mainstream Green movement) but they are, nevertheless, influential.

While the victims' movement remains divided among itself, its power and achievements are necessarily limited by those divisions, but the diversity of organisational forms and of types of service provision is, perhaps, a strength in another sense: if an individual victim or survivor does not feel that one advocacy organisation addresses a particular need, there will often be a choice. The variety of organisations in the field also makes it less likely that the victims' movement will again go quiet on the grounds that its demands have been met: the large organisations are just as involved in the process of expanding their domain as the smaller ones and the more established and powerful groups have a growing number of paid staff and prominent spokespeople with a vested interest in ensuring that they have plenty of work to do. The smaller and more radical groups are in the process of establishing the right to be heard and new groups continue to emerge.

The growing strength of the victims' movement has brought significant benefits to individual victims of crime, both in terms of legal recognition and in the variety and the growing sophistication of types of support available. In the USA the victims' movement is now a powerful political lobby, and this is increasingly the case in Europe too. Perhaps inevitably, the 'official' victims' organisations are more congenial to those in power and find it easier to make their views known, but the growing strength of the movement as a whole means that the more marginal groups are gradually finding ways of putting their points of view to governments and other decision makers. The competition for resources between the 'official' and 'hidden' victims' movements (described in Chapter Four) may be unhealthy but it may mean that, in some instances, the best practices of the feminist and self-help groups are gradually adopted by the more established agencies, and vice versa, to the ultimate benefit of service users.

Work with victims of crime – the future

The implications of the discussion of the pitfalls of inter-agency work and the divisions in the victims' movement will be clear to the reader. On the one hand, the growing diversity of the movement is to be welcomed – but then, the different voluntary agencies are increasingly being forced into competition with each other. They need to find ways of avoiding 'turf wars' – otherwise, energy will increasingly be wasted on defending agency boundaries and competing for funding and recognition rather than responding constructively to victimisation. The statutory agencies have, in some places, found ways of working effectively with the voluntary sector and the lessons of these successes need to be shared more widely so that others are not forced to 'reinvent the wheel'. The police, probation and social services in some areas have developed constructive relationships with a whole range of victim support organisations and their counterparts elsewhere could benefit from this experience being shared. It was clear from the case studies in Chapter Five that one key to such developments is improved staff training; another potentially positive development, if sensitively handled and properly managed, is inter-agency work.

The cynical attempt to use victims' issues for political ends, as discussed in Chapter Four, will become harder to achieve as the victims' movement grows in sophistication. It would be all but impossible if the organisations working with victims of crime, both statutory and voluntary, could reach explicit agreement on many of the issues they already have similar views about. Just as the diverse groups involved in the UK prison reform lobby have joined forces within the Penal Affairs Consortium, so could the agencies concerned with victims' issues make common cause. Like the PAC, such a consortium would need to limit its public statements to issues where all could agree, and this might make for some rather bland pronouncements, but a group representing the police, probation, social services, Victim Support, Women's Aid, Rape Crisis, SAMM and others would be likely to command considerable influence. Such a group could probably agree quite easily on issues which did not make any calls upon its own resources (for example, the need to reform the arrangements for criminal injuries compensation) and, in the longer term, there might be scope for more radical interventions. In the end, political manipulation is only likely to be effectively combated if the victims' movement becomes involved in political debate on its own terms.

The new Crime and Disorder Act has significant implications for work with victims of crime in England and Wales. Local authorities' chief executives have a much strengthened role in co-ordinating crime prevention strategies and they have appointed new, specialist staff in many areas to take this work forward. This is likely to involve bringing the relevant agencies together at local level to agree area-wide strategies and to review the implications of other departments' work for such plans. If taken seriously, these new powers could transform the future of inter-agency work: those engaged in it will become accountable, both to local politicians and to the Home Secretary, and new resources will be needed. The new reparation orders, which will allow courts to require young offenders to make reparation either directly to victims or to the wider community, are being piloted in 1998–99 with a view to national implementation in 2000 (NACRO 1998). If effective methods of inter-agency working are put in place, victims of crime will soon take up a much more central place in the criminal justice system and in the thinking of local authority departments. Where this has occurred in other countries, as, for example, in New Zealand, the role of the victim has been transformed (McElrea 1996; see also Chapter Four).

Although voluntary agencies have made good use of research findings and have often commissioned research themselves (albeit, normally, as part of the process of domain expansion in order to provide evidence of the need for new services), the statutory sector has, in general, been slower to respond to such data. There are obvious exceptions – for example, a good deal of information about hate crimes and their victims is available in the USA because legislation requires that it be collected. Similarly, discrimination within the criminal justice system is monitored under the provisions of the 1991 Criminal Justice Act in England and Wales. The provision of appropriate services, however, is largely left to voluntary groups which use the statistics as part of their case for statutory funding (Jenness 1995).

Powerful research sponsors, such as government departments, respond to political priorities and the commissioning of research thus becomes subject to the same forces which have shaped policies on victims (see Chapter Five). Departments' responses to research findings vary from attempting to censor or suppress them to enthusiastic dissemination and implementation, depending upon political decisions. While this is inevitable, there is also a significant complementary role for the local state in commissioning research and using it to determine priorities, and its spending on victimological research has been increasing. Local crime surveys have become an invaluable aid to policy making (see Chapter One) and local government has often sponsored evaluative research when experimenting with new initiatives in the criminal justice field. Examples discussed in earlier chapters include the Family Violence Court and mandatory charging of domestic violence perpetrators in Winnipeg (Chapter Five), local initiatives on burglary and 'domestic' violence in England (Chapter Two) and new models of inter-agency work by probation and victim agencies (Chapter Four).

Increasingly, such research is more than merely 'administrative' criminology, which tends to be more concerned with patterns of victimisation than with wider social issues (Mawby and Walklate 1994). Nationally-sponsored victimological research has remained preoccupied with questions such as repeat victimisation, which, although undoubtedly an important concern, can fall into the trap of individualising victims' experience and, by implication, blaming them for their victimisation (see Chapters One and Two). Victimology has increasingly moved away from this traditional approach and much of the theoretical and empirical work on responses to male violence, for example, has adopted a more critical approach (see, for example, Hague 1997; Lees 1997; Mawby and Walklate 1994; Mullender 1996; Temkin 1997; Ursel 1997; Walklate 1989).

Critical victimology

This new, critical victimology has exciting possibilities. Making links between criminal victimisation and wider social issues, it offers opportunities for a more sophisticated understanding of crime and the role of victims, and such an understanding may, in turn, facilitate links between the victims' movement and other social movements with overlapping or common aims. Mawby and Walklate (1994), who coined the term and developed the concept, argue that a critical victimology provides evidence and an impetus for a new approach to policy on victims, based upon rights rather than individual needs and upon a notion of victims as citizens rather than passive consumers. Although the state may try to incorporate and co-opt the more radical aspects of the victims' movement, a critical understanding of the forces at work makes this much less likely to occur. What is more, it encourages the formation of links which strengthen the victims' movement and make it more likely to achieve its aims.

The new victimology involves challenging conventional assumptions about citizenship: victims not only have rights but they are part of a struggle with the state to obtain fuller recognition, more rights and a role in defining the terms of the debate (Oliver 1996; Walklate 1998). This includes a challenge to the individualistic and patriarchal assumptions underlying central and much local government policy making: critical criminology is critical because it employs alternative ways of looking at the issues, including collective and feminist approaches, and an examination of the role of the state. It does not automatically put the interests of victims on a pedestal. Instead, 'it considers those policy possibilities which might ensure a more equitable experience of the criminal justice process for all groups of people who might come into contact with it' (Walklate 1998, p.122).

Thus, as in this book, the claims of victims' organisations are themselves examined critically and alongside the issues raised by groups representing other players within the criminal justice system, including the relevant professions and organisations speaking on behalf of offenders. Victims are not idealised – indeed, the insidious nature of the 'ideal type' of a victim is recognised and exposed, as are the overlaps between victims and offenders. The organising principle is a commitment to understanding what would constitute social justice – a consideration all too often omitted from 'administrative' criminology and victimology (Walklate 1998).

Victim support agencies already draw upon feminist ideas and put them into practice in many ways (including parts of the more established and 'official' groups as well as the 'hidden' ones). For example, the ideas of the women's movement have been crucial for the development of self-help women's groups, such as Rape Crisis and Women's Aid, but they have also influenced the nature of the provision made by Victim Support and by police and social services. To a lesser extent, other social movements have also had an impact upon the practice of organisations working with victims. For example, black-led racial harassment projects have shown the need for, and the potential of, community organisation in challenging oppression, but they have also developed practical ways of supporting people victimised because of their race and strategies for preventing repeat victimisation and changing official responses to it, which are of potential use to all agencies working with crime victims. Earlier in this chapter the experience of the American gay and lesbian movement in challenging homophobic violence and supporting its victims was described. Wider alliances are not unthinkable: corporate crime is increasingly being challenged by the environmental movement and trade unions, and victims' organisations may well wish to make contact with such organisations in specific instances. The disability movement has increasingly drawn attention to crime against people with disabilities and has itself been involved in developing a critical understanding of the social construction of disability (Oliver 1996). The possible scope for collaboration with other social movements is huge.

There is a great deal more intellectual work to be done before the insights of critical victimology are fully incorporated into the thinking of agencies working with victims, particularly the more powerful ones. The old, individualistic ways of thinking still dominate and the image of the victim of crime as needy, vulnerable and worthy remains. But the victims' movement itself has begun to challenge these stereotypes and to use critical victimology as a resource. Demeaning language (such as the inappropriate use of the word 'victim' itself) is increasingly challenged and the realisation that categories such as victim and offender are not watertight compartments is coming to inform service provision (even if the overlap between victims and offenders is not yet widely understood). Agencies working with victims are increasingly aware of, and willing to publicise, the connections between criminal victimisation and social disadvantage. It is gradually becoming more difficult for governments to make plans on behalf of victims without consulting at least parts of the victims' movement.

To that extent, the movement has achieved some power. It now needs to find ways to mobilise that strength and to consult its own constituency about how it should be used. The parallel growth of critical victimology offers a potential resource: well-informed decision making depends, to some extent, upon relevant theory and research.

It is clear from the critical research literature that black people, women and children are over-represented as victims of violent crime and that people with disabilities and older people are disproportionately likely to be the victims of financial abuse (see Chapter Two). This evidence alone offers an ambitious agenda for future service provision by the statutory and voluntary victim support sectors and for campaigning work by the latter, perhaps in collaboration with existing specialist charities and campaign groups.

The victims' movement is part of a wider set of struggles for social justice. It has the potential to be co-opted by the state and to abandon its weaker adherents, but it also has enormous positive potential. Critical victimology offers some of the tools needed to realise that potential.

Landmarks in Support for Victims of Crime

1963	Statutory compensation scheme for victims of crime introduced in New Zealand
1964	Criminal Injuries Compensation Board set up in the UK
1966	First community service by offenders scheme set up in the USA
1969	First conditional diversion of offenders scheme set up in Devon, England
1970	First national victimisation survey conducted in Finland
1971	Statutory compensation for victims established in Sweden
1972	Criminal Justice Act; compensation orders without any application being made by the victim introduced in England and Wales; Community Service Orders introduced experimentally in England
1972	First UK Women's Aid refuge set up in Chiswick, London
1972	Statutory compensation for victims established in Austria
1972–75	National Victims' Association (later renamed Victim Support) and the first Victim Support scheme established in Bristol, England
1974/5	First American and Canadian experiments in victim-offender mediation
1975	Community Service Orders introduced permanently in England and Wales

1975   Experimental victim support schemes set up in the Netherlands by Humanitas, a voluntary probation project

1976   National Organization for Victim Assistance (NOVA) established in the USA

1976   Limited protection of identity of raped women introduced in courts in England and Wales

1976   First UK Rape Crisis centre set up, in London

1976   Compensation schemes set up in the Netherlands, Norway and Denmark

1977   Compensation scheme set up in France

1981   Crime Victims Benefit Payment Law came into effect, providing compensation to victims of violence and survivors of homicide victims in Japan

1982   Roger Graef's film on Thames Valley Police treatment of women reporting rape first shown on TV in England

1982   Criminal Justice Act; compensation as a penalty in its own right introduced in England and Wales

1982   Victim Witness Protection Act; introduced penalties for interfering with witnesses, and mechanisms for victims to express their views about sentencing (USA)

1982   Victim Offender Reconciliation Program began in British Columbia, Canada, bringing victims and young offenders together to reach agreement about restitution

1983   South Yorkshire Probation's victim/offender mediation experiment started (UK)

1983   Council of Europe adopted the *Convention on State Compensation* for victims of violent crime

1983   Ministry of Justice encouraged the development of local victim support schemes in France

1984   Victims of Crime Act and Justice Assistance Act (USA) introduced central government funding and the use of courts' fines income to finance victim support

1984   Landelijk Organisatie Sclachtofferhulp (national victim support agency) set up in the Netherlands

1985   General Assembly of the United Nations adopted the *Declaration of the Basic Principles of Justice for Victims of Crime and Abuse of Power*

1985   Experimental mediation and reparation projects set up in England to work with serious offenders

1986   National Institute for Assistance for Victims (INAVEM) created to co-ordinate sixty local victim support associations in France

1986   Childline telephone advice service for children introduced in the UK

1986   Victim Protection Act increased victims' rights to participate in the criminal justice system in Germany

1986   Duluth, Minnesota Domestic Abuse Intervention Project publishes its programme's training manual for use elsewhere; pilot schemes set up in other countries

1987   First national government funding for Victim Support in England and Wales

1987   Victims of Offences Act introduced victim impact statements to sentencing process in New Zealand

1988   Criminal Justice Act; courts required to give reasons for not ordering compensation; video links in child abuse cases introduced in England and Wales

1988   Home Office Circular 20/1988; chief constables asked to keep victims informed and produce leaflets about compensation and pass information on losses to Crown Prosecution Service in England and Wales

1988   Legislation required police and prosecution in the Netherlands to keep victims informed and arrange restitution (introduced experimentally in 1993, then nationally in 1995)

1988   Legislation in Canada and South Australia introduced victim impact statements prior to sentencing of offenders

1989   CHANGE programme established in Scotland; court-ordered re- education programme for men who are convicted of violence towards their partners

1989   Humanitas established restitution and conflict resolution projects in the Netherlands

1989   Children, Young Persons and their Families Act established Family Group Conferences in New Zealand, bringing young offenders and their victims together and giving victims an effective say in sentencing decisions

1990   Victim's Charter (England and Wales)

1990   Home Office Circular 59/1990 instructs police to take victims' views into account when considering the cautioning of offenders in England and Wales

1990   Lothian Domestic Violence Probation Project established in Edinburgh, Scotland; see CHANGE above

1990   Specialist family violence court established in Winnipeg, Canada, aimed at quicker and more rigorous sentencing, and at protecting victims

1991   Criminal Justice Act; compensation to be collected and passed on before fines; videotaped evidence in child abuse cases introduced in England and Wales

1991   Victim Assistance Act increased victims' rights to participate in the criminal justice system, and to receive compensation, in Switzerland

1992   'Zero Tolerance' publicity campaign against male violence, Edinburgh, Scotland

1992   Sentencing circles first used officially to involve local communities in making decisions about offenders and victims in Aboriginal communities in Canada

1992   Uniform Victims of Crime Act requires American probation officers to try and ascertain victims' views about the sentencing of offenders

1994   Home Office Probation Circular 77/1994: 'Contact with victims and victims' families', implementing the provisions of the Victim's Charter in England and Wales

1995   Victims in the Netherlands given legal right of appeal where police and prosecutors act against their expressed wishes

1995   New National Standards for pre-sentence reports on offenders include requirement to take victims' views into account when probation officers advise courts in England and Wales

1995   Victim Support UK publishes *The Rights of Victims of Crime*

1996   Victim's Charter, revised edition, for England and Wales

1996   National network of Victim/Witness Support schemes in place in Crown Courts in England and Wales; experimental schemes began in Scottish courts

1996   National Police Agency introduces Assistance for Crime Victims Policy, providing information and counselling for victims in Japan

1998   Crime and Disorder Act gives local authorities responsibility for crime prevention and introduces reparation orders requiring young offenders to make reparation to victims (where they consent) in England and Wales

Sources: Ashworth 1993; Dobash *et al.* 1996; Holtom and Raynor 1988; Joutsen 1994; Kelly 1990; LaPrairie 1995; Mawby and Walklate 1994; Pence and Paymar 1986; Umbreit 1996; Ursel 1994; Walklate 1989; Wemmers 1996; Wright 1996; Yasuda 1997; Zedner 1994.

References

Amir, M. (1971) *Patterns of Forcible Rape*. Chicago: University of Chicago Press.

Anderson, S., Grove-Smith, C., Kinsey, R. and Wood, J. (1994) *The Edinburgh Crime Survey*. Edinburgh: Scottish Office.

Anderson, S. and Leitch, S. (1996) *Main Findings from the 1993 Scottish Crime Survey*. Edinburgh: Scottish Office Central Research Unit.

Angela (1997) Personal communication with the author from the Manager of North Staffordshire and South Cheshire Rape Crisis, 18 June.

Ashworth, A. (1993) 'Victim Impact Statements and sentencing.' *Criminal Law Review*, July, 498–509.

Association of Chief Officers of Probation (1992) *Position Statement on Domestic Violence*. Wakefield: ACOP.

Association of Chief Officers of Probation (1996) *Probation Services and Victims of Crime*. Position Statement approved by ACOP National Council. Wakefield: ACOP.

Aubrey, C. and Hossack, A. (1994) 'Contacting victims of life sentence crime.' *Probation Journal, 41,* (4), 212–224.

Aye Maung, N. (1993) 'Survey of Victim Support volunteer visitors.' *Home Office Research Bulletin, 34,* 31–35.

Ball, M. (1994) *Funding Refuge Services: a Study of Refuge Support Services for Women and Children Experiencing Domestic Violence*. Bristol: Women's Aid Federation England.

Beck, U. (1992) *Risk Society: Towards a New Modernity*. London: Sage.

Best, J. (1990) *Threatened Children: Rhetoric and Concern about Child Victims*. Chicago: University of Chicago Press.

Blunt, A.P. (1993) 'Financial exploitation of incapacitated: investigation and remedies.' *Journal of Elder Abuse and Neglect 5,* (1).

Bond, H. (1998) 'Support in evidence.' *Community Care*, 1217, 9–15.

Box, S. (1983) *Power, Crime and Mystification*. London: Tavistock.

Brammer, A. (1996) 'Elder abuse in the UK: a new jurisdiction?' *Journal of Elder Abuse and Neglect, 8,* (2), 33–48.

Bridgeman, C. and Sampson, A. (1994) *Wise After the Event: Tackling Repeat Victimisation*. National Board for Crime Prevention, London: Home Office.

Brown, D. J. P. (1993) *A Study of Parents of Murdered Children: Experiences, Reactions and Needs*. Unpublished MA in Counselling dissertation, University of Keele.

Brown, L., Christie, R. and Morris, D. (1990) *Families of Murder Victims Project: Final Report*. London: Victim Support.

Burrell, I. (1998) 'Blair anger at "repugnant" Mary Bell deal.' *The Independent*, 30 April.

Cavadino, M. and Dignan, J. (1990) *The Penal System: An Introduction*. London: Sage.

Carlen, P. (1983) *Women's Imprisonment.* London: Routledge and Kegan Paul.

Carmody, M. (1991) 'Invisible victims: sexual assault of people with an intellectual disability.' *Australia and New Zealand Journal of Developmental Disabilities 17,* 2, 229–36.

Chan, J.B.L. (1997) *Changing Police Culture: Policing in a Multicultural Society.* Cambridge: Cambridge University Press.

Christie, N. (1986) 'The ideal victim' in E. A. Fattah (ed) *From Crime Policy to Victim Policy: Reorienting the Justice System.* New York: St. Martin's Press.

Christie, N. (1993) *Crime Control as Industry.* London: Routledge.

Clarke, R., Ekblom, P., Hough, M. and Mayhew, P. (1985) 'Elderly victims of crime and exposure to risk.' *Howard Journal 24,* 1, 1–9.

Community Care (1998) Reports of conference on 'A Fair Hearing: Justice for People with Learning Difficulties.' 19–25 February.

Cook, D. and Hudson, B. (eds) (1993) *Racism and Criminology.* London: Sage.

Cowburn, M., Wilson, C. and Loewenstein, P. (1992) *Changing Men: a Practice Guide to Working with Adult Male Sex Offenders.* Nottingham: Nottinghamshire Probation Service.

Crawford, A., Jones, T., Woodhouse, T. and Young, J. (1990) *Second Islington Crime Survey.* London: Middlesex Polytechnic Centre for Criminology.

Cretney, A. and Davis, G. (1995) *Punishing Violence.* London: Routledge.

Croall, H. (1992) *White Collar Crime.* Buckingham: Open University Press.

Dobash, R., Dobash, R.E., Cavanagh, K. and Lewis, R. (1996) 'Re-education programmes for violent men.' *Research Findings 46,* Home Office Research and Statistics Directorate.

Dobash, R. E. and Dobash, R. (1979) *Violence against Wives.* London: Open Books.

Dominelli, L., Jeffers, L., Jones, G., Sibanda, S. and Williams, B. (1995) *Anti-Racist Probation Practice.* Aldershot: Arena.

Drakeford, M. and Vanstone, M. (eds) (1996) *Beyond Offending Behaviour.* Aldershot: Arena.

Elias, R. (1986) *The Politics of Victimisation.* Oxford: Oxford University Press.

Elias, R. (1990) 'Which victim movement?' In A. J. Lurigio, W.G. Skogan and R. C. Davis (eds) *Victims of Crime: Problems, Policies and Programs.* Newbury Park: Sage.

Elias, R. (1993) *Victims Still.* London: Sage.

Elias, R. (1994) 'Has victimology outlived its usefulness?' *Journal of Human Justice 6,* 1, 4–25.

Erikson, K. (1976) *Everything in its Path: Destruction of Community in the Buffalo Creek Flood.* New York: Simon and Schuster.

Farrell, G. and Pease, K. (1993) *Once Bitten, Twice Bitten: Repeat Victimisation and its Implications for Crime Prevention.* Crime Prevention Unit Paper 46, London: Home Office.

Fattah, E.A. (1979) 'Some recent theoretical developments in victimology.' *Victimology 4,* (2), 198–213.

Fattah, E.A. (ed) (1986) *From Crime Policy to Victim Policy.* Basingstoke: Macmillan.

Fattah, E.A. and Sacco, V.F. (1989) *Crime and Victimization of the Elderly.* New York: Springer-Verlag.

Fenwick, H. (1995) 'Rights of victims in the criminal justice system: rhetoric or reality?' *Criminal Law Review,* November.

FitzGerald, M. and Hale, C. (1996) *Ethnic Minorities: Victimisation and Racial Harassment.* Home Office Research Study 154. London: Home Office.

Forrester, D., Frenz, S., O'Connell, M. and Pease, K. (1990) *The Kirkholt Burglary Prevention Project: Phase II.* Crime Prevention Unit Paper 23. London: Home Office.

Genn, H. (1988) 'Multiple victimization.' In M. Maguire and J. Pointing (eds) *Victims of Crime: a New Deal?* Milton Keynes: Open University Press.

George, M. (1998) 'Safe havens.' *Community Care,* 12–18 March, 12.

Hague, G. (1997) 'Smoke screen or leap forward: interagency initiatives as a response to domestic violence.' *Critical Social Policy 17,* (4), 93–109.

Hague, G., Malos, E. and Dear, W. (1996) *Inter-Agency Approaches to Domestic Violence.* Bristol: University of Bristol, School for Policy Studies.

Hanmer, J. and Stanko, E. (1985) 'Stripping away the rhetoric of protection: violence to women, law and the state in Britain and the USA.' *International Journal of the Sociology of Law 13,* 357–74.

Hartcliffe and Withywood Black Support Group (1993) *Standing Out: to be Black in Hartcliffe and Withywood.* Bristol: Barnardo's.

Hartless, J.M., Ditton, J., Nair, G. and Phillips, S. (1995) 'More sinned against than sinning: a study of young teenagers' experience of crime.' *British Journal of Criminology 35,* (1), 114–133.

Heidensohn, F. (1968) 'The Deviance of Women: a Critique and an Enquiry.' *British Journal of Sociology 19,* (2).

Heilbron Committee (1975) *Report of the Advisory Group on the Law of Rape.* London: IIMSO, Cmnd. 6352.

Her Majesty's Inspector of Constabulary (1997) *Masefield's Progress: How Heavy is the Administrative Burden on the Police Now?* Report of a Thematic Inspection. London: Home Office.

Her Majesty's Inspectorate of Probation (1998) *Exercising Constant Vigilance: the Role of the Probation Service in Protecting the Public from Sex Offenders.* Report of a Thematic Inspection. London: Home Office.

Holtom, C. and Raynor, P. (1988) 'Origins of victims support philosophy and practice.' In M. Maguire and J. Pointing (eds) *Victims of Crime: a New Deal?* Milton Keynes: Open University Press.

Home Office (1964) *Compensation for Victims of Crimes of Violence.* Cm 2323. London: HMSO.

Home Office (1990) *Victim's Charter: a Statement of the Rights of Victims of Crime.* London: Home Office Public Relations Branch.

Home Office (1996) *The Victim's Charter: a Statement of Service Standards for Victims of Crime.* London: Home Office Communications Directorate.

Home Office (1996a) *Probation Service Training Materials for Contact with Victims.* London: Home Office Probation Training Section.

Hood, T. (1997) 'Witness support within Staffordshire: the role of Witness Care – a localised response to a national issue.' Unpublished dissertation submitted as part of the BSc Policing and Police Studies course, University of Portsmouth.

Hood, T. (1998) (Inspector in the Criminal Justice Administration Department, Staffordshire Police) Personal interview with the author, 6th April.

Hough, M. and Mayhew, P. (1983) *The British Crime Survey*. London: HMSO.

Hudson, B. and Galaway, J. (1996) (eds) *Restorative Justice: International Perspectives*. Amsterdam: Kugler.

Hugman, R. (1994) *Ageing and the Care of Older People in Europe*. Basingstoke: Macmillan.

Jenkins, P. (1997) *Counselling, Psychotherapy and the Law*. London: Sage.

Jenness, V. (1995) 'Social movement growth, domain expansion and the framing process: the gay/lesbian movement and violence against gays and lesbians as a social problem.' *Social Problems 42*, (1), 145–170.

Johns, R. and Sedgewick, A. (1999) *Law for Social Work Practice: Working with Vulnerable Adults*. Basingstoke: Macmillan.

Jones, D. (1996) 'Tough on crime and nasty to children.' *Prison Report 36*, Autumn, 4–5.

Jones, G.M. (1987) 'Elderly people and domestic crime.' *British Journal of Criminology 27*, (2), 191–201.

Jones, T., MacLean, B. and Young, J. (1986) *The Islington Crime Survey*. Aldershot: Gower.

Joutsen, M. (1987) *The Role of the Victim of Crime in European Criminal Justice Systems*. Helsinki: Helsinki Institute.

Joutsen, M. (1994) 'Victimology and victim policy in Europe.' *CJ Europe 4*, (5), 9–12.

Kelly, D. (1990) 'Victim participation in the criminal justice system.' In A. J. Lurigio, W. G. Skogan and R. C. Davis (eds) *Victims of Crime: Problems, Policies and Programs*. Thousand Oaks: Sage.

Kelly, L., Burton, S. and Regan, L. (1996) 'Beyond victim or survivor: sexual violence, identity and feminist theory and practice.' In L. Adkins and V. Merchant (eds) *Sexualizing the Social: Power and the Organization of Sexuality*. Basingstoke: Macmillan.

Kingston, P. and Penhale, B. (1995) *Family Violence and the Caring Professions*. Basingstoke: Macmillan.

Kinsey, R. (1984) *Merseyside Crime Survey*. Liverpool: Merseyside Metropolitan Council.

Kinsey, R. and Anderson, S. (1992) *Crime and the Quality of Life: Public Perceptions and Experience of Crime in Scotland*. Edinburgh: Scottish Office.

Kirby, M. (1995) *Investigating Political Sociology*. London: Collins.

Kitzinger, J. and Hunt, K. (1993) *Evaluation of Edinburgh District Council's Zero Tolerance Campaign*. Edinburgh: Edinburgh District Council Women's Committee.

Knox, J. (1996) 'A prison perspective.' In K. Cavanagh and V.E. Cree (eds) *Working with Men: Feminism and Social Work*. London: Routledge.

Koffman, L. (1996) *Crime Surveys and Victims of Crime*. Cardiff: University of Wales Press.

Kosh, M. and Williams, B. (1995) *The Probation Service and Victims of Crime: A Pilot Study*. Keele: Keele University Press.

LaPrairie, C. (1995) 'Altering course: new directions in criminal justice – sentencing circles and family group conferences.' *Australian and New Zealand Journal of Criminology*, 78–99.

Lees, S. (1996) *Carnal Knowledge.* London: Hamish Hamilton.

Lees, S. (1997) *Ruling Passions: Sexual Violence, Reputation and the Law.* Buckingham: Open University Press.

Levi, M. (1994) 'Violent crime.' In M. Maguire, R. Morgan and R. Reiner (eds) *The Oxford Handbook of Criminology.* Oxford: Clarendon.

Loader, I. (1996) *Youth, Policing and Democracy.* London: Macmillan.

London Rape Crisis Centre (1984) *Sexual Violence: the Reality for Women.* London: LRCC.

Luckasson, R. (1992) 'People with mental retardation as victims of crime.' In R. W. Conley, R. Luckasson and G. N. Bouthilet (eds) *The Criminal Justice System and Mental Retardation: Defendants and Victims.* Baltimore: Brookes.

Lupton, C. (1994) 'The British refuge movement: the survival of an ideal?' In C. Lupton and T. Gillespie (eds) *Working with Violence.* Basingstoke: Macmillan.

Lupton, C. (1998) 'User empowerment or family self-reliance? The family group conference model.' *British Journal of Social Work 28,* (1), 107–128.

McElrea, F.W.M. (1996) 'The New Zealand Youth Court: a model for use with adults.' In B. Galaway and J. Hudson (eds) *Restorative Justice: International Perspectives.* Amsterdam: Kugler.

MacLeod, M. D., Prescott, R. G. W. and Carson, L. (1996) *Listening to Victims of Crime: Victimisation Episodes and the Criminal Justice System in Scotland.* Edinburgh: HMSO.

McShane, M. D. and Williams, F. P. (1992) 'Radical victimology: a critique of the concept of victim in traditional victimology.' *Crime and Delinquency 38,* (2), 258–71.

Maguire, M. (1980) 'The impact of burglary upon victims.' *British Journal of Criminology 20,* (3), 261–75.

Maguire, M. (1994) 'Crime statistics, patterns and trends.' In M. Maguire, R. Morgan and R. Reiner (eds) *The Oxford Handbook of Criminology.* Oxford: Clarendon.

Maguire, M. and Bennett, T. (1982) *Burglary in a Dwelling.* London: Heinemann.

Maguire, M. and Corbett, C. (1987) *The Effects of Crime and the Work of Victim Support Schemes.* Aldershot: Gower.

Mann, R. (1996) 'Reducing the risk of sexual reoffending.' In J. Braggins and C. Martin (eds) *Managing Risk: Achieving the Impossible.* Report of ISTD's 1995 Annual Residential Conference. London: Institute for the Study and Treatment of Delinquency.

Marchant, C. (1993) 'Negative outlook: counselling – women in prison', *Community Care,* 11 March, 24.

Markus, E. (1997) Personal correspondence with author.

Marsh, P. and Crow, G. (1998) *Family Group Conferences in Child Welfare.* Oxford: Blackwell.

Marshall, T.H. (1975) *Social Policy in the Twentieth Century, 4th ed.* London: Hutchinson.

Masters, R., Friedman, L.N. and Getzel, G. (1988) 'Helping families of homicide victims: a multidimensional approach.' *Journal of Traumatic Stress 1,* (1), 109–25.

Mawby, R.I. (1988) 'Age, vulnerability and the impact of crime.' In M. Maguire and J. Pointing (eds) *Victims of Crime: a New Deal?* Milton Keynes: Open University Press.

Mawby, R.I. and Gill, M.L. (1987) *Crime Victims: Needs, Services and the Voluntary Sector.* London: Tavistock.

Mawby, R.I. and Walklate, S. (1994) *Critical Victimology*. London: Sage.

Mayhew, P., Aye Maung, N. and Mirrlees-Black, C. (1993) *The 1992 British Crime Survey*. Home Office Research Study no 132, London: HMSO.

Mayhew, P., Elliott, D. and Dowds, L. (1989) *The 1988 British Crime Survey*. Home Office Research Study no 111, London: HMSO.

Meier, S. T. and Davis, S. R. (1993) *The Elements of Counseling*, 2nd ed. Pacific Grove: Brooks/Cole.

Mendelsohn, B. (1956) 'Une nouvelle branche de la science bio-psycho-sociale: victimologie.' *Revue Internationale de Criminologie et de Police Technique*, 10–31.

Mezey, G. (1988) 'Reactions to rape: effects, counselling and the role of health professionals.' In M. Maguire and J. Pointing (eds) *Victims of Crime: a New Deal?* Milton Keynes: Open University Press.

Midwinter, E. (1990) *The Old Order: Crime and Older People*. London: Centre for Policy on Ageing.

Miers, D. (1989) 'Positivist victimology: a critique.' *International Review of Victimology* 1, (1), 3–22.

Morgan, J. and Zedner, L. (1992) 'The Victim's Charter: a new deal for child victims?' *Howard Journal* 31, 4, 294–307.

Morgan, J. and Zedner, L. (1992a) *Child Victims: Crime, Impact and Criminal Justice*. Oxford: Clarendon.

Morris, A. (1987) *Women, Crime and Criminal Justice*. Oxford: Oxford University Press.

Morris, A., Maxwell, G. M. and Robertson, J. P. (1993) 'Giving victims a voice: a New Zealand experiment.' *Howard Journal of Criminal Justice* 32, (4), 304–321.

Moxon, D. (1993) 'Use of compensation orders in magistrates' courts.' *Research Bulletin* 25, Home Office.

Mullender, A. (1996) *Rethinking Domestic Violence: the Social Work and Probation Response*. London: Routledge.

Mullender, A. and Ward, D. (1991) *Self-directed Groupwork: Users Take Action for Empowerment*. London: Whiting & Birch.

Murray, I. (1998) Personal communication with the author from Training Co-ordinator of Rape Crisis Federation, Wales and England, 29 April.

National Association for the Care and Resettlement of Offenders (1998) *The Crime and Disorder Bill*. NACRO Briefing leaflet, London: NACRO.

National Association of Probation Officers (1997) *Victim Perspectives and Victim Contact Work*. Policy Document PD 3–97, London: NAPO.

National Association of Victim Support Schemes (1988) *The Victim in Court: report of a Working Party*. London: NAVSS.

Nettleton, H., Walklate, S. and Williams, B. (1997) *Probation Training with the Victim in Mind: Partnership, Values and Organisation*. Keele: Keele University Press.

Newburn, T. (1993) 'The long-term impact of victimisation.' *Home Office Research Bulletin 33*, 30–34.

Newburn, T. (1997) 'Youth, crime and justice.' In M. Maguire, R. Morgan and R. Reiner (eds) *The Oxford Handbook of Criminology, 2nd ed*. Oxford: Clarendon.

Newburn, T. and Stanko, E. A. (1994) 'Introduction: men, masculinities and crime.' In T. Newburn and E. A. Stanko (eds) *Just Boys Doing Business*. London: Routledge.

Newburn, T. and Stanko, E.A. (1994a) 'When men are victims: the failure of victimology.' In T. Newburn and E.A. Stanko (eds) *Just Boys Doing Business*. London: Routledge.

Newburn, T. (1995) *Crime and Criminal Justice Policy*. Harlow: Longman.

Normandeau, A. (1968) 'Patterns in robbery.' *Criminologica*, 6.

Nuttall, M. and Morrison, S. (1997) *It Could Have Been You*. London: Virago.

Oliver, M. (1996) *Understanding Disability: from Theory to Practice*. Basingstoke: Macmillan.

Owen, H. and Pritchard, J. (1993) *Good Practice in Child Protection*. London: Jessica Kingsley Publishers.

Pallister, D. (1996) 'Criminals win compensation for abuse in childhood after appeal to injuries board.' *The Guardian*, 16 August.

Parkes, C.M. (1993) 'Psychiatric problems following bereavement by murder or manslaughter.' *British Journal of Psychiatry 162*, 49–54.

Parkins, S.M. (1996) 'Hospital responses to elder abuse: the adult protective team.' In A. Baumhover and S.C. Beall (eds) *Abuse, Neglect and Exploitation of Older Persons*. London: Jessica Kingsley Publishers.

Parliamentary All-Party Penal Affairs Group (1996) *Increasing the Rights of Victims*. London: PAPPAG.

Parton, N. (1996) 'Social work, risk and the "blaming system".' In N. Parton (ed) *Social Theory, Social Change and Social Work*. London: Routledge.

Pearce F. and Tombs, S. (1993) 'Union Carbide and Bhopal.' In F. Pearce and M. Woodiwiss (eds) *Global Crime Connections: Dynamics and Control*. London: Macmillan.

Pease, K. (1997) 'Crime prevention.' In M. Maguire, R. Morgan and R. Reiner (eds) *The Oxford Handbook of Criminology, 2nd ed.* Oxford: Clarendon.

Peelo, M., Stewart, J., Stewart, G. and Prior, A. (1992) *A Sense of Justice: Offenders as Victims of Crime*. Wakefield: Association of Chief Officers of Probation.

Pence, E. and Paymar, M. (1986) *Power and Control: Tactics of Men Who Batter, an Educational Curriculum*. Duluth, Minnesota: Minnesota Program Development Inc.

Perry, J. (1993) *Counselling for Women*. Buckingham: Open University Press.

Philpot, T. (1997) 'Eager for change.' *Community Care*, 4–10 September, 26–27.

Phipps, A. (1988) 'Ideologies, political parties and victims of crime.' In M. Maguire and J. Pointing (eds) *Victims of Crime: a New Deal?* Milton Keynes: Open University Press.

Pithers, B. (1993) *Promoting Victim Empathy in Sadistic Offenders*. (video) Coventry: University of Warwick.

Platek, M. (1995) 'What it's like for women: criminology in Poland and Eastern Europe.' In N.H. Rafter and F. Heidensohn (eds) *International Feminist Perspectives in Criminology: Engendering a Discipline*. Buckingham: Open University Press.

Plotnikoff, J. and Woolfson, R. (1998) *Options for Improved Support for Victims and Other Witnesses Attending Magistrates' Courts*. London: Home Office.

Pritchard, J. (1992) *The Abuse of Elderly People*. London: Jessica Kingsley Publishers.

Radford, J. and Stanko, E.A. (1991) 'Violence against women and children: the contradictions of crime control under patriarchy.' In K. Stenson and D. Cowell (eds) *The Politics of Crime Control*. London: Sage.

Raine, J.W. and Smith, R.E. (1991) *The Victim/Witness in Court Project: Report of the Research Programme*. Birmingham: University of Birmingham.

Raine, J.W. and Walker, B. (1990) 'Quality of service in the Magistrates' Courts.' *Home Office Research Bulletin 28.*

Rape Crisis Federation, Wales and England (undated) 'Values Statement', poster. Nottingham: RCF.

Reeves, H. and Wright, M. (1995) 'Victims: towards a reorientation of justice.' In D. Ward and M. Lacey (eds) *Probation: Working for Justice.* London: Whiting and Birch.

Roeher Institute/L'Institut Roeher (1995) *Harm's Way: the Many Faces of Violence and Abuse against Persons with Disabilities.* North York, Ontario: Roeher Institute.

Saini, A., Fleming, J. *et al.* (1997) *'So What's the Point of Telling Anyone?' – a Black Community Perspective on Crime in the Leicester City Challenge Area.* Leicester: Centre for Social Action, De Montfort University.

Sampson, A. and Phillips, C. (1995) *Reducing Repeat Racial Victimisation on an East London Estate.* Police Research Group Paper no. 67. London: Home Office.

Sanders, A., Creaton, J., Bird, S. and Weber, L. (1997) *Victims with Learning Disabilities: Negotiating the Criminal Justice System.* Oxford: University of Oxford Centre for Criminological Research.

Sarkis, A. and Webster, R. (1995) *Working in Partnership: the Probation Service and the Voluntary Sector.* Lyme Regis: Russell House.

Saulsbury, W. and Bowling, B. (1991) *The Multi-Agency Approach in Practice: the North Plaistow Racial Harassment Project.* London: Home Office Research and Planning Unit, paper no.64.

Schulman, P. W. (1997) *A Study of Domestic Violence and the Justice System in Manitoba.* Winnipeg: Commission of Inquiry into the deaths of Rhonda Lavoie and Roy Lavoie.

Schwarz, J. (1991) Review of E. Fattah and V.F. Sacco (1989) *Crime and Victimization of the Elderly.* New York: Springer Verlag. In *International Review of Victimology 2*, 1, 73–4.

Scott, A. (1990) *Ideology and the New Social Movements.* London: Routledge.

Shakespeare, T. (1996) 'Power and prejudice: issues of gender, sexuality and disability.' In L. Barton (ed) *Disability and Society: Emerging Issues and Insights.* Harlow: Longman.

Slapper, G. (1994) 'Crime without Punishment.' *The Guardian*, 1 February. Reprinted in J. Muncie and E. McLaughlin (eds) *The Problem of Crime.* London: Sage.

Smart, C. (1977) *Women, Crime and Criminology.* London: Routledge and Kegan Paul.

Smith, A. (1993) 'British line up to join anti-male campaign.' *Sunday Times*, 24 January.

Smith, D. (1995) *Criminology for Social Work.* Basingstoke: Macmillan.

Smith, D., Paylor, I. and Mitchell, P. (1993) 'Partnerships between the independent sector and the Probation Service.' *Howard Journal 32*, (1), 25–39.

Sobsey, D. (1994) *Violence and Abuse in the Lives of People with Disabilities: the End of Silent Acceptance?* Baltimore: Brookes.

Sparks, R., Genn, H. and Dodd, D. (1977) *Surveying Victims.* Chichester: Wiley.

Staffordshire Trials Issues Group (1997) *A Local Service Level Agreement on Responsibilities for Victims and Witnesses.* Stafford: STIG.

Stanko, E.A. (1988) 'Hidden violence against women.' In M. Maguire and J. Pointing (eds) *Victims of Crime: a New Deal?* Milton Keynes: Open University Press.

Stewart, J., Smith, D., Stewart, G. and Fullwood, C. (1994) *Understanding Offending Behaviour.* Harlow: Longman.

Strobl, R. (1997) 'Theoretical and Empirical Arguments for a New Concept of the Victim.' Paper presented at the ninth International Symposium on Victimology, Amsterdam, August.

Support After Murder and Manslaughter (1997) *Annual Report 1996/97.* London: SAMM.

T., Anna (1988) 'Feminist responses to sexual abuse: the work of the Birmingham Rape Crisis Centre.' In M. Maguire and J. Pointing (eds) *Victims of Crime: a New Deal?* Milton Keynes: Open University Press.

Temkin, J. (1996) 'Doctors, rape and criminal justice.' *Howard Journal* 35, 1, 1–20.

Temkin, J. (1997) 'Plus ça change: reporting rape in the 1990s.' *British Journal of Criminology 37*, (4), 507–528.

Travis, A. (1994) 'Home Office tackles wife battering.' *The Guardian*, 25 October.

Trials Issues Group (1996) *Statement of National Standards of Witness Care in the Criminal Justice System.* London: TIG.

Tritter, J. (1994) 'The Citizen's Charter: opportunities for users' perspectives?' *Political Quarterly 65*, (4), 397–414.

Troyna, B. and Hatcher, R. (1992) 'It's only words: understanding "racial" and racist incidents.' *New Community 18*, 3, 493–6.

Umbreit, M.S. (1996) 'Restorative justice through mediation: the impact of programs in four Canadian provinces.' In B. Galaway and J. Hudson (eds) *Restorative Justice: International Perspectives.* Amsterdam: Kugler.

Ursel, E.J. (1994) 'The Winnipeg Family Violence Court.' *Juristat 14*, (12), May.

Ursel, E.J. (1997) 'The Possibilities of Criminal Justice Intervention in Domestic Violence: a Canadian Case Study.' *Current Issues in Criminal Justice 8*, (3), 263–274.

Ursel, E.J. (1998) 'Mandatory charging: the Manitoba model.' In K. Bonneycastle and E. Rigakos (eds) *Unsettling Truths: Battered Women, Policy, Politics and Contemporary Research in Canada.* Vancouver: Collective Press.

Victim Support (1990) 'Rights and Responsibilities.' Editorial. *Victim Support,* September.

Victim Support (1995) *The Rights of Victims of Crime.* London: Victim Support.

Victim Support (1996) *Annual Report 1995.* London: Victim Support.

Victim Support (1996a) *Women, Rape and the Criminal Justice System.* London: Victim Support.

Victim Support (1997) *Annual Report 1996.* London: Victim Support.

von Hentig (1948, reprinted 1967) *The Criminal and His Victim.* Evanston, Illinois: Archon.

Walklate, S. (1984) *SLVSS: a Consumer Evaluation.* Liverpool: Liverpool Polytechnic, Crime Justice and Welfare Unit.

Walklate, S. (1986) 'Reparation: a Merseyside view.' *British Journal of Criminology 26*, 287–298.

Walklate, S. (1989) *Victimology: the Victim and the Criminal Justice Process.* London: Unwin Hyman.

Walklate, S. (1996) 'Equal opportunities and the future of policing.' In F. Leishman, B. Loveday and S. P. Savage (eds) *Core Issues in Policing.* Harlow: Longman.

Walklate, S. (1998) *Understanding Criminology: Current Theoretical Debates.* Buckingham: Open University Press.

Waxman, B.F. (1991) 'Hatred: the unacknowledged dimension in violence against disabled people.' *Sexuality and Disability 9,* 3, 185–99.

Webster, C. (1995) 'Youth crime, victimisation and racial harassment.' Paper in *Community Studies no. 7,* revised edition, Ilkley: Centre for Research in Applied Community Studies, Bradford and Ilkley Community College.

Weed, F.J. (1995) *Certainty of Justice: Reform in the Crime Victim Movement.* New York: Aldin de Gruyter.

Wemmers, J.M. (1996) *Victims in the Criminal Justice System.* Amsterdam: Kugler.

Wemmers, J.M. and Zeilstra, M.I. (1991) 'Victims services in the Netherlands.' *Dutch Penal Law and Policy 3,* The Hague: Ministry of Justice.

West Midlands Probation Service Sex Offender Unit (1996) *Sex Offender Groupwork Programme.* Birmingham: West Midlands Probation Service.

Whalen, M. (1996) *Counseling to End Violence against Women: a Subversive Model.* London: Sage.

Widom, C.S. (1991) 'Childhood victimization: risk factor for delinquency.' In M.E. Colton and S. Gore (eds) *Adolescent Stress: Causes and Consequences.* New York: Aldine de Gruyter.

Williams, B. (1996) *Counselling in Criminal Justice.* Buckingham: Open University Press.

Williams, B. (1996a) 'The probation service and victims of crime: paradigm shift or cop-out?' *Journal of Social Welfare and Family Law 18,* (4), 461–474.

Williams, B. (1997) *The Victim's Charter: Citizens as Consumers of Criminal Justice Services.* Unpublished paper given at the conference on 'Citizenship and the Welfare State: Fifty Years of Progress?' at Ruskin College, Oxford on 18–19 December.

Williams, B. (forthcoming 1999) 'Initial education and training for social work with victims of crime.' *Social Work Education.*

Williams, B. (forthcoming 1999) 'Focus on victims.' In B. Beaumont (ed) *Work with Offenders: a Progressive Approach.* Basingstoke: Macmillan.

Williams, C. (1995) *Invisible Victims.* London: Jessica Kingsley Publishers.

Wilson, M. (1996) 'Working with the CHANGE men's programme.' In K. Cavanagh and V.E. Cree (eds) *Working with Men: Feminism and Social Work.* London: Routledge.

Wolfgang, M.E. (1958) *Patterns in Criminal Homicide.* Philadelphia: University of Pennsylvania Press.

Women's Aid Federation England (1992) *Report to the Home Affairs Committee Inquiry into Domestic Violence.* Bristol: WAFE.

Wright, M. (1996) 'Can mediation be an alternative to criminal justice?' In B. Galaway and J. Hudson (eds) *Restorative Justice: International Perspectives.* Amsterdam: Kugler.

Yasuda, T. (1997) 'The present situation of the police-led assistance program for crime victims in Japan.' Unpublished paper given at the 9th International Symposium on Victimology, Amsterdam, August.

Yorath, M. (1995) 'Managing murder.' *Police Review 18* August, 26–7.

Young, J. (1988) 'Risk of crime and fear of crime: a realist critique of survey-based assumptions.' In M. Maguire and J. Pointing (eds) *Victims of Crime: a New Deal?* Milton Keynes: Open University Press.

Young, J. (1994) 'Recent paradigms in criminology.' In M. Maguire, R. Morgan and R. Reiner (eds) *The Oxford Handbook of Criminology.* Oxford: Clarendon.

Zedner, L. (1994) 'Victims.' In M. Maguire, R. Morgan and R. Reiner (eds) *The Oxford Handbook of Criminology.* Oxford: Clarendon.

Zedner, L. (1997) 'Victims.' In M. Maguire, R. Morgan and R. Reiner (eds) *The Oxford Handbook of Criminology.* 2nd ed. Oxford: Clarendon.

Index

Assault 29, 30, 127

Australia 35, 39, 142

Burglary 9, 24, 25, 44, 46, 52–4, 104, 126, 134

Canada 36, 39, 50, 85, 100, 102, 104, 118–21, 134, 139, 140, 142

Child abuse 18, 45, 48–9, 50, 94–6, 126, 141

Childline 45

Class 29, 32, 46–8, 49, 54, 128, 131, 137

Compensation 15, 17, 49, 62, 64–5, 71, 76–7, 79, 92, 107, 128, 139, 140, 141, 142

Confidentiality 12, 72, 86, 95, 114

Crimes of the powerful 28–9, 46, 136

Courts 12, 18, 33, 39, 54, 56, 64, 76, 79, 91, 92, 96, 107, 116, 118–21

Disabled victims 31, 35–9, 102, 108, 109, 116, 136, 137

'Domestic' violence 14, 20, 22, 26, 29, 30, 32–3, 47, 50, 70, 76, 85, 96–8, 104, 105, 108, 111, 114, 118–21, 123, 125, 134, 142

Elias, Robert 14, 15, 19, 28, 68–70, 81, 83, 94

Fear of crime 40–41

Feminism 17, 21, 33, 34, 69, 72, 84, 87, 94, 97, 135–6

France 11, 104, 140, 141

Hate crimes 31, 36, 128, 129, 130, 134

Home Office 11, 13, 17, 50, 69, 71, 75, 83, 87, 91, 94, 96, 99, 102, 103, 106, 115

Homophobia 31, 34–5, 113, 136

Housing departments 26, 74, 90, 96

'Ideal' victims 19, 70, 126–7, 136

Inter-agency work 11, 20, 33, 37, 50, 72, 73, 85, 89, 93, 96, 97, 111, 115, 116, 117–121, 123–5, 133–4

Ireland 11

Japan 100, 140, 143

Law 15, 69, 74, 76, 77, 80, 86, 88, 99, 102, 111, 133

Local crime surveys 20

Medical model of disability 38

Men as victims 34

Murder 9, 12, 18, 21, 49, 54–60, 76, 91, 98–9, 101, 108, 113

NACRO 11

Netherlands 11, 15, 117, 140, 141, 142, 143

New Zealand 83, 134, 139, 141, 142

Northern Ireland 11

Offenders 15, 48–50, 55, 60, 63, 67, 68, 77–9, 80–3, 85, 98, 110, 111, 112, 126–8, 137, 139

Older victims 40–3, 104

Poland 17

Police 11, 17, 18, 20, 24, 25, 26, 29, 33, 35, 36, 37, 43, 55–6, 59, 61–3, 70, 73, 75, 76, 79, 86, 92–3, 95, 96, 100–106, 119, 125, 136, 141, 142

Politicisation of victim's issues 7, 9, 12, 13, 14, 67–88, 133

Post-traumatic Stress 52, 55, 58, 65, 126

Probation Service 11, 55, 57, 59–60, 70, 76, 77–9, 82–3, 96, 98, 106, 107, 109–16, 119, 120, 124, 125, 126, 143

Prosecution Services 29, 35–6, 62, 76, 79, 106–9, 141

Racial harrassment and Violence 14, 20, 25–7, 29–32, 47, 70, 73, 76, 90, 101, 113, 136, 137

Rape 9, 12, 14, 15, 17, 18, 26–7, 33, 49, 60–5, 76, 90, 92–6, 99, 101, 103, 104, 106, 108, 114, 140

Rape Crisis Centres 10, 15, 21, 45, 48, 61, 65, 69, 70, 72, 84, 86, 87–8, 93–6, 110, 113, 115, 124, 136, 140

Repeat victimisation 20, 23–6, 29, 54, 102

Restorative justice 81, 83, 140, 142

Risk 30, 112, 114

Robbery 17, 46, 117

SAMM 10, 55, 57–9, 84–5, 98–9

Scotland 11, 12, 109, 142

Sexual abuse 38, 44, 45, 47, 52, 70, 80, 91, 101, 112

Social services departments 11, 37, 45, 70, 96, 124

Survivors 21, 55–6, 58, 97, 98, 113, 137

Theft 32, 37, 43, 44, 46

Training 11, 12, 36–7, 39, 45, 55, 72, 82, 86, 87, 105, 109, 113, 116, 121, 123

USA 14, 35, 36, 37, 81, 83, 85, 97, 99, 100, 109, 128, 129, 132, 139, 140, 141, 142

Victim-blaming 8, 16–19, 23–4, 33, 37–8, 111

Victimology 16–9, 134
  critical 19–21, 28, 135–7

Victim Support 10, 11, 13, 15, 22, 25–6, 42, 44, 45, 48, 52–3, 55, 57, 59, 62–5, 69, 70, 71, 72, 73, 75, 76, 79, 84, 86, 87, 89, 90–3, 94, 97, 98, 101, 102, 105, 110, 113, 115, 124, 125, 129, 130, 131, 139, 141, 143

Victim surveys 20, 29, 33–4, 47

Victim's Charter 8, 9, 57, 67, 74–83, 88, 103, 106, 107, 110, 126, 131, 142, 143

Victim's Movement 9, 10, 69, 76, 78, 80, 85, 128–32, 135

Volunteers 9, 11, 25–6, 50, 86–7, 90, 91, 96, 99, 114

Women as victims 32–5, 61, 137

Women's Aid 10, 15, 22, 48, 69, 72, 80, 84, 86, 87, 89, 96–8, 110, 113, 115, 124, 131, 136, 139

Young people 27, 43–6, 101, 128, 137

Zero tolerance 50, 85, 104, 134, 142